To Joyce with best wishes,

Buddy Thompson

11/22/83

Madam
BELLE
Brezing

This picture was made in Mullen's Studio in Lexington. Belle Brezing's dress was probably as fine as those of the wealthiest women of Kentucky at the time. Her hair appears very light, probably red.

Madam BELLE Brezing

by Buddy Thompson

Buggy Whip Press

1983

Buggy Whip Press

121 Park Avenue
Lexington, Ky. 40508

ISBN: 0-9612824-0-1 (Cloth)
ISBN: 0-9612824-1-X (Leather)
Library of Congress Catalog Card Number: 83-72950

Jacket Design: Lois Johannigman
Pen and Ink Illustrations: Carole Konther Granai
Book Design: Ed Houlihan

Printed by the C. J. Krehbiel Co.
Cincinnati, Ohio

Foreword

The excitement which surrounded the publication of Margaret Mitchell's *Gone With the Wind* in 1936 enveloped all of America and much of the world. Hollywood producers immediately began to vie for movie rights to the story; actors and actresses worked to perfect a Southern drawl in the hope that they might be selected to play a coveted part in what promised to be to filmdom what the book was to literature.

In Lexington, Kentucky, just about everyone recognized the elegant character of Belle Watling as that of the now aged Belle Brezing, who had been queen of the city's red light district at the turn of the century. Indeed, many parallels could be drawn in addition to the shared first name: both ran fancy brothels; both last names had the same number of syllables and ended in "ing." Lexington men who had known her "personally" felt, too, that their Belle was just the kind of good "ole" whore who would have befriended the likes of Rhett Butler.

The clincher, many thought, was that Mitchell's husband, John Marsh, a Maysville, Kentucky, boy, had attended the University of Kentucky in Lexington from 1926 to 1929 and, while a student, had worked as a reporter at *The Lexington Leader*.

Belle Brezing had already reached the status of a local folk legend, and no one could be convinced that Marsh had not furnished his wife with the name and some of the attributes of the character that became Belle Watling in *Gone With the Wind*.

The book and subsequent movie led to a great interest in "Belle-mobilia." Joe Jordan, a Lexington newspaper writer, who for years had frequently referred to Belle in his daily column and on his local radio program, began a file devoted to the now famous madam. When the movie became a box office smash, Lexington's interest increased.

Jordan, seeking reassurance on the Brezing-Watling connection, wrote John Marsh, asking if the character of Belle Watling had not, in fact, been modeled after Belle Brezing.

Marsh wired back:

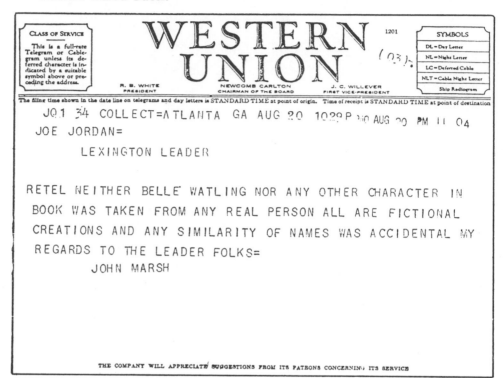

This was the only possible answer at the time, of course, since Belle was still living and could conceivably have filed suit. Jordan did not believe Marsh. He knew the similarities between the two women were too great to be accidental, but the telegram must have disappointed him. *Gone With the Wind* was receiving worldwide attention, and any tie-in with Belle Brezing would have assured the success of anything Jordan wrote.

J. C. "Skeets" Meadors, the well-known horse photographer, also became interested in Belle and began his own collection. When Belle died in 1940, both men pillaged the trash heaps in the backyard of Belle's house as workers carried out boxes of old papers and photographs in preparation for an auction of the contents. They found numerous early pictures of Belle and her girls, as well as photographs of her establishment, inside and out. Unfortunately, most of the pictures had been torn in two as they were discarded. Several of her account books were ripped apart and the pages torn. There were people still living who were pictured here and whose names appeared in the ledgers, and the crew setting up the sale intended to destroy all such evidence of the past. Jordan also acquired the scrapbook Belle had kept as a girl.

More important, they interviewed several older women who, in their youth, had "boarded" at Belle's and spoke to old patrons of the establishment, who gave graphic descriptions of the operations, the "inmates" (girls), and the customers of the bawdy house that flourished through the Gay Nineties and well into the twentieth century.

Based on the voluminous information they had obtained, Jordan and Meadors considered collaborating on a book; and others showed interest in their work. A. B. Guthrie, who was at that time Executive Editor of *The Lexington Leader*, received a letter from R. E. Banta, the book publisher, asking for information and pictures relating to Belle and her house and stating that he would be interested in seeing a manuscript on the madam's life. Since Guthrie was about to board a train for New York to see a publisher about his forthcoming book, *The Big Sky*, and knew that Jordan probably had more information about the madam than anyone else at the paper, he asked Jordan, who was City Editor, to write to Banta. Jordan's first draft of the letter, which was included with the Jordan/Meadors collection, indicates he went into some detail; however, before typing the final letter, he eliminated several paragraphs. The original version reads, in part:

> I got to digging around, had some good luck right at the start that encouraged me to keep on. That fall in New York I was talking to Ruth and Maxwell Aley, literary agents whom you may know. They had handled some stuff for me. I got to telling them about Belle, more because I was interested in the topic than because I had any idea of doing anything with it. They got pretty excited, because they had been buying some movie rights for Selznick, who produced "Gone" and he had told them he would like a story in which to star Munson, the gal who played B. Watling. What, they wanted to know, would be better for her than the life story of the original Belle? They got Doubleday interested to the extent that they assigned Clara Claasen (who edits Ken Roberts' books), to work with me, with the idea of publishing a book.

However, Jordan was called into the Navy soon after this and had a "fairly rugged time." He was in Naval hospitals twice on Pacific islands and three times back in the states. After he left the service, he was hospitalized three additional times with what he said "the doctors called nervous exhaustion."

Margaret Mitchell and John Marsh came to Lexington from Maysville on the L. & N. train on November 28, 1940; and Burton Milward, a reporter for *The Lexington Leader* who later became City Editor, was at the old Union Station when the train pulled in. He asked if he might interview the author and was invited to accompany the couple to the hotel, where Mitchell graciously answered his questions. She denied knowing of Belle Brezing when she wrote Watling into her book.

Anne Edwards' book, *Road to Tara*, published by Ticknor & Fields, 1983, states on page 150 and in a footnote reference that among Margaret Mitchell's other worries was the fact that she had copied Belle Watling's character after Belle Brezing of Lexington, Kentucky, whom John had described to her. I called Mrs. Ben Marsh, Margaret Mitchell's sister-in-law, and mentioned the Edwards' book and its statement regarding Brezing. Mrs. Marsh said Margaret Mitchell had told her personally that she had never heard of Belle Brezing until after she wrote *Gone With the Wind*.

On June 6, 1983, I wrote Edwards and asked her if she could give me information regarding the matter. Her reply of July 12, 1983, reads, in part:

> Belle Breezing is certainly worthy of a biography and I find it most interesting that you are writing one. Despite the Marshes' denial that the lady was the model for Belle Watling, Margaret Mitchell did research points in Miss Breezing's life and mentions her in early letters to Frances Marsh (John Marsh's sister) during the writing of *Gone With the Wind*. In one she remarks that there was probably a woman like Belle Breezing "entertaining" soldiers during the Civil War as Belle Breezing did during the First World War. She also makes note of Belle Breezing's dyed red hair (which she said a colleague of John's told her about).
>
> When *Gone With the Wind* was published, Belle Breezing was alive and Margaret Mitchell was always terrified of being sued for libel.

I have been told that John Marsh, speaking in Lexington several years ago to the veterans of the Barrow Unit, stated that he furnished his wife with the character of Belle Brezing as the basis for Belle Watling. I was able to reach only one surviving member of the Barrow Unit; he informed me that he had not been able to attend that reunion.

John Marsh's telegram was sent while Belle Brezing was still living. Burton Milward's interview with Margaret Mitchell took place two months after Brezing died, but there is no way of knowing if Marsh or his wife knew of the madam's death. It certainly appears that John Marsh and Margaret Mitchell felt a denial was imperative while Belle Brezing was still alive and later stuck to their original story.

Based on the number of similarities and the information from Edwards, Belle Brezing was undoubtedly used as a prototype for Belle Watling.

More books remain in the minds of men than ever reach the press; and Jordan, whose disabilities had forced him to leave the newspaper, realizing he would never write Belle's story, sold Meadors his collection. The photographer asked that the purchase be kept confidential, since he did not want to be bothered by those now becoming interested in Belle, among them many would-be authors and collectors. To all who asked, Jordan said that the collection had been sold to a man in California.

Meadors' wife Gladys typed all the original interviews. Although Meadors, like Jordan, never got around to writing Belle's story, he did seek help by writing to Rear Admiral Gene Markey, outlining his idea and sending, by Warren Wright, Jr. (Markey's stepson), copies of all his material and pictures. Markey, who was the husband of Calumet Farm owner Lucille Parker Wright Markey, spent his summers in Lexington and was well-known to Meadors through their horse connections. The Admiral was certainly the man with the background and Hollywood contacts to help with the project. Before his marriage to Mrs. Wright, he had wed and divorced screen stars Joan Bennett, Hedy Lamarr, and Myrna Loy. He had spent ten years in Hollywood as producer and writer and was the author of a number of books, including a historical novel based in part in the Lexington area.

Markey wrote:

Dear Skeets:

Young Warren gave me your notes and photographs on Belle Breezing. You have certainly dug up some material on the Old Girl—and, with the photographs, it should make an extremely good article or, possibly a short book. You realize, of course, that there are many gaps to be filled in—and these can only be done by an experienced writer who can amplify the atmosphere of a bordello in those lusty times. Are you considering doing this job yourself—or with the help of a collaborator? I don't quite know what to suggest as I have no idea who would be available in Lexington. But I don't doubt that there are some capable writers, with a bent for history, around the universities. . . .

I wish you well with the project—and if I can be of any help in suggesting how you proceed, I shall be most happy. I am returning the notes and photographs herewith.

Sincerely,
Gene Markey

Markey had not taken the bait, and it was back to Meadors if anything was to be done.

Meanwhile, the fascination with Belle among Lexingtonians never waned. Women whose mothers and grandmothers had been Belle's severest critics took great pride in any item that had come from "the big house on the hill." Men who knew their fathers only as unyielding disciplinarians wondered if they had ever been human enough to have sought the secret delights of the girls at Miss Brezing's house of disrepute. Only a few years before, Belle's name would never have been spoken in a parlor or in the presence of ladies; now the mention of her and her girls provoked only amusement. People from all walks of life bought any item purported to have come from Belle's mansion, and unscrupulous antique dealers sold anything Victorian or gaudy as a genuine artifact from the famous bawdy house. The stigma had vanished with time and the changing moral climate.

Meadors made other attempts to find a collaborator, but was unsuccessful. However, he continued garnering scraps of Belle's life up until the time of his death in 1967. Later, his wife Gladys worked with the notes and interviews, but was unable to find anyone interested in writing the story. Some fifteen years later, she decided to dispose of the collection. It came as a great surprise that the material had been in Lexington all these years, and I immediately acquired the lot.

The Jordan/Meadors collection had no information on Belle's background other than her mother's name and a few facts on her early childhood. Jordan had assumed (as have several others) that Belle's mother was first married to McMeekin and later to Brezing. Research proved this to be incorrect.

Other small collections were obtained, some from people who would be considered most unlikely to have been interested in Miss Belle. In one instance, only after a brutal murder came the disclosure that Brezing notes and anecdotes were among the murdered man's papers.

In each collection, many items were only notations, scraps with names or dates; but each offered a small lead. Tedious research discounted some, while others provided another piece to the puzzle of a life that started before the Civil War, when few records were kept.

Added to these collections are the fruits of several years of research into old records in libraries, courthouses, cemeteries, archives, and attics throughout Kentucky, as well as a complete search through newspaper files. Soon the material which had begun with the Jordan/Meadors collection more than doubled in size. Three other collections of material were borrowed, and numerous persons who had known Belle or had firsthand information on her life were interviewed. Research was done in other states. Numerous items in the original collection were found to be in error. Dates were wrong, and names were incorrect. Frequently, misspelled names in old newspapers and court and cemetery records further confused the project. Brezing was often Breezing, Bresin, Brezin, Breazing, Brezzing, or Bresing (throughout her life, Belle alternated between using one or two "e's" in Brezing; I have elected to use one "e" since this was her more frequent use); Cook was sometimes Koch; Cox was often written Cocks; Kenney was Kinney, and so on, making the search more difficult.

Often jokes or stories had been "personalized"; many times the same stories were found to have been told about madams and prostitutes in other areas. Perhaps some originated with Belle or "on the hill," but they have not been included unless authenticated on independent grounds.

All of this material was first arranged in chronological order and indexed. In the case of interviews that covered a number of subjects and persons, copies were made and the references cross indexed and arranged according to subject. A separate file was set up on each person whose life touched Belle's. Dozens of pictures were studied, and discoveries were made that added new information. These files not only aided in further research and writing, but also sometimes rendered startling new facts when put into proper sequence.

Several pamphlets have been published regarding Belle. These, along with often-told stories and references in the newspapers, have contained gross inaccuracies. Frequently, the question is asked, "Was she black or mulatto?" The truth is she was Caucasian, with dark brown hair and fair complexion. She stood under five feet in height; and her weight, judging from her pictures, probably was less than one hundred pounds. Other inaccuracies will not be individually addressed; but the facts, based on research, can dispel the misinformation and finally give a true story of her life and times.

I have pored over all available records, read and reread dozens of interviews, and talked personally with many people who knew her. After over two years of such concentrated work, I feel as though I knew her personally, rather than just having caught fleeting glimpses, as is the true case. I am now confident I know how she would have reacted to almost every situation.

In order to impart this acquired insight, I have at times reported conversations that were undoubtedly held, but have myself supplied the detailed dialogue: this in order to set the scene and to help the reader better understand the time, the place, and the people. Such insertions have not altered the facts in any way. By the same token, I have taken the liberty of describing Belle's feelings at some of the crises in her life.

I discovered I had a great deal of sympathy for this girl who found herself ostracized through no fault of her own and who, based on her reaction (sometimes rash, perhaps) to circumstances beyond her control, was forced to take the only course left open to her. It might be argued that her sister Hester grew up in the same atmosphere, but had married and had, as far as we know, a very respectable life with a husband and children. But here we must admit that siblings in many families adjust differently to adversity and follow opposite paths in life. After half a century, there are those still ready to judge her without a thought of how hard her life might have been and what they might have done given the same circumstances. I have been accosted by several persons who feel the story of a prostitute should not be written. To them, of course, I will not devote space for comment.

Others whose help has been indispensable I wish to gratefully recognize: *Burton Milward*, whose time was freely given and whose files and remarkable memory of Lexington history were a tremendous aid; *Mrs. A. R. Musser*, whose lifelong interest in the history of Lexington has been enlightening, as well as pleasurable to me; *Mrs. A. R. McMurtry* and *Mrs. Linda Ashley*, for their genealogical research; *Dr. John L. Cutler*, for his corrections to the manuscript; *John C. Wyatt*, for his assistance in acquiring the Jordan/Meadors collection and for his aid in copying old photographs and photographing other items; *Mr. and Mrs. E. B. Sparks*, who, together with Mrs. Sparks' late father, owned the old Megowan Street house from the time it was sold out of Belle's estate; *Mrs. Gladys Meadors*, who, I hope, will enjoy seeing the fruits of her late husband's work in print; the staff at *Lexington Cemetery* and *Mrs. Mary Margaret Sullivan* of *Calvary Cemetery* for their assistance in finding graves and burial information; *Joe Murphy* and *Mary Genevieve Townsend Murphy*, who furnished the information gleaned by Mrs. Murphy's late father, the beloved *William H. Townsend*; *Bobby True*, Circuit Clerk, *Mrs. Dorothy Beard*, and *Mrs. Bobbie Harris* of the Fayette County Circuit Clerk's Office, for obtaining old records from the archives at Frankfort; *Dr. Hambleton Tapp* and *Dr. James C. Klotter* and others at the *Kentucky Historical Society*, for the assistance given me; *Bettye Lee Mastin*, whose interest in Lexington history has been of great value to the community, as well as to me; the *Margaret I. King Library*, University of Kentucky, and its staff; the *Transylvania University Library*; *Arthur Lawson* and the staff at the *Lexington Public Library*; *Mr. and Mrs. John Tuska*, whose reaction to stories told helped me judge their interest for inclusion; *William I. Goodwin* and *Robert F. Watts*, for information and firsthand accounts of the auction of Belle's estate; *Lawrence T. Flynn*, who clerked the sale of Belle's personal property in 1940 and kindly recollected the situation for me; the late *J. Winston Coleman, Jr.*, who was interested in the project and gave aid and counsel; *Joseph C. Graves, Jr.*, who furnished pictures of the Megowan Street house made just prior to its demise; *Bettie Kerr*, for her valuable research; *Mrs. Flora Hudson* and her daughter *Ruth Hudson*, who gave me pertinent information regarding 153 North Eastern Avenue; *Mrs. Bernice Bottom*, who furnished books from her collection on the Victorian period; *James W. McNeil*, who has an abiding interest in Belle, shared some of his information, and discussed his findings with me; *Anne Edwards*, author of *Road to Tara*, for her help in regard to the Brezing-Watling dispute; *A. C. Stagg*, for the loan of his Brezing material; *Foster Ockerman, Jr.*, for legal interpretations concerning Belle and the statutes; *Charles L. Calk* and *Carl Timothy Cone*, for advice and counsel; *Don Edwards, Will Murphy*, and *Mrs. Sue Wylie*, for their interest; *The Lexington Herald-Leader*, for permission to reprint articles; *Bob and Lois Johannigman*, for their contribution; *Mrs. Carole Konther Granai*, for her drawings and art work; *Ed Houlihan*, for his advice and aid in arrangements for publication; *Richard DeCamp*, for his advice on publishing; *Edith Mongan*, who aided tremendously in organizing the files, deciphering my longhand original manuscript, and typing each of several revised manuscripts; my son, *Joseph Clay Thompson*, for his constructive criticism, editing, and interest in my work; and my wife, *Mildred (Peg) Campbell Thompson*, who helped me find uninterrupted time to work and has shared my interest in history, antiques, and old houses.

I have purposely left out the names of those who gave me first-hand information that might cause them embarrassment; but I am thankful to them, also.

What follows represents the essence of a great deal of work started several decades ago by Joe Jordan and Skeets Meadors, who are to be highly credited; for without their early interest, much of this material would have been lost.

To avoid the distraction of footnotes, a separate section has been set aside at the end of the text to provide necessary explanations and list sources and contributions.

Introduction

She was born the illegitimate child of a prostitute in a little rented house at the edge of Lexington in 1860, and she died in 1940 only a few blocks away in the shambles of what had been her "gilded mansion for men."

As a bastard child in a small town with Victorian principles, she irritated the community by her very existence. At twelve she was seduced by a married man nearly three times her age, who correctly thought no one would care. Her reputation at fourteen, when she found herself pregnant, was already so bad that the newspaper felt free to ridicule her with reference to "La Belle," to the great amusement of its readers, who had certainly heard stories of her. She married and separated in a week; and a few months later, she bore the child conceived with another man before her marriage.

Destitute and almost without hope, she became a prostitute to support her child. But somewhere inside her tiny frame was a spark of defiance which she fanned into flaming action that carried her to the top of the life that had been forced upon her.

In her heyday, she stirred a constant cry of outrage by driving through town with the finest horses hitched to the grandest carriage. Beautifully dressed as she always was on these outings, she seemed to the women of Lexington to be the embodiment of a dangerously attractive evil.

She was known in New York as the small, attractive Southerner, Mrs. Kenney, who visited the city periodically to stay in the best hotels and buy a selection of the latest and finest Paris fashions.

Her generosity to the needy and her support of charitable causes was often rejected by a community which resented gifts that overshadowed their token pie and cake sales.

While she (understandably) failed with women, she excelled with men. She knew senators, congressmen, governors, and great men of commerce — on a first-name basis. One of the wealthiest men of the century helped her buy a house and build it into an establishment costing much more than most men made in a lifetime; and when two Kentuckians delivered thoroughbred horses to South America, they were approached in a fashionable restaurant by gentlemen who, hearing they were from Lexington, asked about Miss Belle.

She was indicted more often than any other citizen of the town, but she never served an hour in jail. If the charge resulted in a fine, she paid it; if it was more serious, she was defended by the best lawyers, who were authorized to draw checks on her account and pay whatever was necessary to settle the matter. On at least one occasion, she received dismissal of grand jury charges and clemency by order of the governor of the state.

At the end, though, most of her adversaries were dead; and the city that had once despised her read her obituary, along with those of world celebrities, in *Time* magazine.

MILESTONES

Died. William Meade Lindsley Fiske III, 29, famed U. S. winter-sportsman, driver of winning Olympic bobsleds (1928, 1932), reputedly the first American to join the R. A. F. as a pilot; of wounds received during aerial combat; somewhere in southeastern England. In 1938 Mr. Fiske married the beauteous Countess of Warwick.

Died. Walter P. Chrysler, 65, locomotive wiper who became one of the three greatest automobile producers in the U. S.; after long illness; in Great Neck, Long Island. Son of a railroad engineer, Machinist Chrysler in 1905 bought an automobile with $700 savings, a $4,300 loan, kept taking it apart and reassembling it until he found what made it tick. In 1911 he resigned a $12,000-a-year job as general manager of American Locomotive Co. to work for Buick at half the pay. Two-fisted, paternal Tycoon Chrysler drove himself and his men, thought "the one reasonably sure way to get ahead was to do just a little bit more than was expected of you." Two salvage jobs he did on moribund companies—Willys-Overland and Maxwell Motor Corp.—led to the birth of Chrysler Corp., which boomed even in the depression. In 1933 Chrysler outproduced Ford for the first time; same year Chrysler stock multiplied seven times in value.

Died. Franklin Henry Hooper, 78, editor emeritus of the Encyclopaedia Britannica; of injuries when he was hit by a truck; in Saranac Lake, N. Y. After supervising five *Encyclopaedia* editions as managing or U. S. editor, he became editor-in-chief in 1932, retired two years ago. A dauntless pedestrian, Editor Hooper persistently flouted traffic signals, replied to friends' pleas for caution: "We are all going to die some day."

Died. John Eliot Wolff, 82, professor emeritus of geology at Harvard University; of thirst and exhaustion; in the Mojave Desert, California. Motoring across the desert (where the heat often reaches 120°) for a one-day camping trip, Geologist Wolff apparently got stuck in the sand. While awaiting death or rescue, Professor Wolff wrote a codicil to his will, leaving a bequest to his gardener.

Died. Belle Breazing, about 82, famed Kentucky bawd; in Lexington, Ky. Her plushy, luxurious salon, famed for its influential patrons and for being the most orderly of disorderly houses, was closed by the U. S. Army in 1917, when Camp Stanley was set up on the outskirts of Lexington. Day after Miss Breazing's death, the Lexington *Herald* ran her obit on the front page. All copies were sold by 10 a.m., brought private speculators $1 apiece, provoked many a caustic phone call (Sample: "Is it true that to get on the front page of the *Herald* one must operate a house of ill repute?").

TIME, August 26, 1940

CHAPTER 1

Born To Rejection

Mary Belle was born June 16, 1860, to Sarah Ann Cox, a single woman who had borne another illegitimate child, Hester, six years earlier. The three lived in a small rented house on Rose Street, just off Main, in Lexington, Kentucky, with Sarah's kinsman, Elias Cox. Elias was a farm laborer who had come to Fayette County with Sarah from neighboring Woodford County following the death of his father, John Cox.

"Kinsman" is used here since the exact relationship between Sarah Ann and Elias is difficult to discern from available records. The settlement of John Cox's estate following his death in 1849 states he left no widow, but the following children: Elias and Rebecca Cox, both of Woodford County; Enoch of Anderson County; Sarah Ann, the wife of William Carr of Mercer County; and Timothy, who had moved to Indiana.

The 1850 Woodford County census lists the family as Elias Cox, age 49; Rebecca Cox, 60; and Sarah A. Cox, 14. Since Elias and Rebecca were brother and sister, and they had a sister named Sarah Ann who was already married, this younger Sarah Ann was not a sister; and no records indicate that Rebecca or Elias had ever taken a spouse. If she was the child of either, Sarah, like her daughters, was illegitimate.

The 1860 Fayette County census lists Elias Cox, age 56; Sallie (Sarah Ann) Cox, 24; and Hester Cox, 6. This census was taken June 5th and 6th; Belle was not born until June 16th.

Hester's birth was recorded March 2, 1852. Her mother was listed as Sarah Cox, father as "unknown"; the notation "Illegitimate" appears under "Remarks." This, of course, indicates that Elias and the younger Sarah, although living together in the same house, were not husband and wife.

It may plausibly be assumed that Sarah Ann (Belle's mother) was Rebecca Cox's illegitimate daughter, but this is only speculation.

That Sarah, Elias, and the two small children came from a poor background is evident from a look at the existing records of the Cox family. John Cox, Elias' father, was a Revolutionary War veteran, who had enlisted in Rowan County, Virginia, in 1781, and served one year in Captain Alexander Brevard's 2nd North Carolina Regiment in the Continental Establishment, under Colonel Dixon, with General Greene as Commander-in-Chief. He fought in the Battle of Eutaw Springs, saw action in the Siege of Ninety Six (a town in North Carolina), and was discharged near the line between North and South Carolina in 1782.

In 1822, he made application for a pension under the law of 1818. His sworn statement said, in part, that he was fifty-nine years of age and "I can work tolerable well for one of my age." He listed his total assets as:

Two horses one old & one young	worth	$43.00
Two cows & two calves	worth	$20.00
Poultry		$1.00
Farm utensils		$6.00
House furniture [besides one bed allowed under the pension act]		$40.00
Kitchen furniture		$4.00
		$114.00

He was allowed a pension of eight dollars a month, paid semiannually. The Powhatan County, Virginia, records seem to indicate that John's first wife was Susannah, whom he married in 1788, and that by her he had Enoch and Rebecca. After Susannah's death, he married Elizabeth White, a younger woman, who was the mother of his other children: Elias, Sarah Ann, and Timothy. Elizabeth died, and he was a widower at the time of his death.

None of the family could read or write. There is no indication they ever owned land or even a house. In the slavery times of Kentucky, they were little better off than the blacks; and though not in bondage, they were reduced to a hand-to-mouth existence, working as farm laborers when work was available.

When John died on February 19, 1848, he had evidently lost what little he had in 1822; his entire estate consisted of the next-due pension check. After all expenses were paid (including eight dollars for his coffin), his five children shared what remained, each receiving $4.48. It was shortly after the old man died that Elias and Sarah moved to Lexington.

The sheriff of Woodford County reported to the court on his efforts to collect taxes for 1831, with the following results as regards the Cox family: Elias Cox — no estate; Enoch Cox — insolvent; and William Carr, who had married the first Sarah Ann — moved to Mercer County before the sheriff got there.

Elias, who, like his father, worked as a hired hand, disappeared soon after Mary Belle was born. He appears in no census or tax record after 1860, and his burial place cannot be found in any Lexington or Woodford County cemetery. Perhaps he tired of living with this wanton woman; or perhaps, if Sarah was his niece, he had "tasted of forbidden fruit" and decided when the second child was born that it was time to clear out.

On December 16, 1861, when Mary Belle, or "Belle," as she was called, was a year old and Hester was seven, their mother married George Brezing. Although Sarah professed the Catholic faith, she and Brezing were married by a Baptist minister. The children assumed the Brezing name, although they were not legally adopted. Brezing, a German immigrant who came to Lexington shortly before the marriage, operated a saloon on Water Street.

Not long after the marriage, the new family took up residence on West Main Street in a small brick house a few doors west of Jefferson, and Brezing opened a grocery at the corner.

Known in the community as a short-tempered man given to "bouts with the bottle," Brezing was generally disliked by his neighbors and even his customers, who bought from him only because of the convenience of his store. Sarah was also given to heavy drink; and this, with the knowledge of her two illegitimate children, made the Brezings unacceptable to families in the area. Parents warned their children not to be seen with, or to play with, Hester or Belle.

The two lonely little girls grew up in the turmoil of a home where both stepfather and mother were frequently drunk. In these drunken fits, the couple would fight, curse, smash dishes, and destroy furniture.

Brezing would often leave home and spend the night in a bawdy house. His wife, not to be outdone, would dress up and venture out to some saloon, leaving the two young girls to fend for themselves. Sarah occasionally returned with a man she had picked up and would take him to bed in a room adjacent to the one the frightened children shared. The impressions left on Belle at this early age can only be imagined.

When sober, however, Sarah made beautiful dresses for the girls and assured them of her love. These rare moments must have been the few rays of sunshine that gleamed through an otherwise dismal existence. Miss Linda Neville, who lived on West Main Street in the same block as the Brezings, recalled later that Belle and Hester were always "very well dressed."

While Hester attended the old No. 2 School across the street, a forlorn little Belle would stand at the window, awaiting her sister's return. She had no one else to play with; mothers of neighboring children saw to that.

Old No. 2 School (Harrison School) on West Main Street across from Belle's early childhood home.

Brezing periodically tried to better his financial situation by buying property, but was always on the brink of foreclosure. As his losses and, inevitably, his drinking increased, he became more antagonistic toward Sarah. Eventually, many people were afraid to enter his store after witnessing the frequent altercations between them. He would throw things and physically abuse her when customers were present; and at home, the children would become hysterical at his threats to kill their mother with a pistol or knife.

Belle eagerly looked forward to her first day at school. At last she would have friends, youngsters her own age to play with. She had watched the children at the school across the street at recess and almost felt she was part of their games. She was sure she would be better at "Blindman's Bluff" than the little girls who seemed always to go in the wrong direction. When she and Hester jumped rope, they had tied one end to the fence since there was never a third child to hold the other end. Now she would "run in" with two of her playmates to hold the jump rope. She promised herself she would study hard and bring home stars on her report card and get the little "Reward of Merit" slips — Ma would be so proud of her.

Hester might have prepared Belle for what to expect. She had been in school six years and would no longer be in Harrison School across the street when Belle started. This would be her first year in Dudley School, way over on Maxwell Street. She had gone through the agony of being ignored; but when she was finally told that the other children were not allowed to play with her, she wilted. Each day, she carried the pain like a stone in her chest as she went to face another day of being alone in a crowd of children.

Note the spelling of Belle's name on the "Reward of Merit."

Belle was told the first day, by a child too young to understand the reason, that her mother had told her she would get a whipping if she played with her. Belle was a bright child; before the last bell, she knew all the children had been told the same.

If Belle had been shy and as easily crushed as Hester, perhaps her entire life would have been different; but she was not. Each slight was repaid with a curse. She knew the words that her mother and stepfather used when they fought, and her vocabulary in that category was substantial.

Dudley School, on the corner of Maxwell and Mill Streets. The second school Belle attended.

Soon the teacher found Belle to be more of a problem than all the rest of the class. She occasionally overheard one of Belle's choice epithets and was forced to discipline her, which each time brought a defiance hardly expected from so tiny a girl. And to compound the problem, there were the mothers who let it be known that they did not want their children slighted because of the constant time taken up with "that Brezing brat."

If a question was asked of the class, Belle would be called only if hers was the only hand up; and the teacher always selected the hardest word for Belle in the spelling bee, fearful that she would win and be put at the top of the class. That would have been hard to explain to indignant parents.

Notes sent home by the teacher or principal were answered in a childish hand. Since Sarah could neither read nor write, and Brezing only in German, Hester, now in the seventh grade, handled the correspondence.

Knowing the Brezings' reputation, the teacher feared to stop across the street to discuss Belle. The only hope was that the child would quit school; certainly no one would object or try to make her come back. But Belle would not give up. She would say what she wanted, and do what she wanted, and "to hell with all of you!"

It must have been hard for Belle to decide whether being at school with its problems or at home with the brawling was easier.

She worked twice as hard to get one of the "Reward of Merit" slips that were freely given to others.

Finally, as things got worse at home, Sarah filed for divorce in March of 1866; Brezing entered a countersuit. At the time, a divorce was considered almost as scandalous as the other things Sarah had done. The testimony was so lewd that it became the talk of the town. A few excerpts from the case file, now in the archives at Frankfort, Kentucky, will attest to the character of both Brezing and Sarah.

James R. Heatherington testified that he saw Sarah and another woman in McGurke's Coffee House Saloon (Water Street), drinking together, and that the women went into the back room of the saloon with McGurke, H. Kearns, and Heatherington. McGurke and Sarah then went upstairs, stayed a short while, and returned. According to Heatherington, there was only a mattress in the upstairs room. Kearns and Sarah later went to the room and remained there together a short time before returning to the others. They all then had another drink before separating, McGurke going home with Sarah at about eleven o'clock. Heatherington stated it was understood that when the couples went upstairs they intended to have sexual intercourse. He added that the woman with Sarah that night was known to him as a common prostitute.

Heatherington further testified that he met Sarah once in broad daylight at a house kept by a Mrs. James on Broadway, which was known to be a "house of ill fame." He also indicated he had seen Sarah on the street with other men on different occasions drinking and in an intoxicated condition. He concluded that he was "satisfied that her conduct has been such as to indicate her to be a woman of ill fame and unchaste."

John Wurth testified he had seen Sarah with another woman at Cooke's Beer Saloon. The two women arrived about eight o'clock. Someone paid for their drinks, and Sarah drank one glass after another until she had had about seven or eight drinks. According to Wurth, Sarah scattered the beer all over the room so that others had to leave. Both women then went out after Brezing "to take him on." When they returned with him in about half an hour, Sarah bought drinks all around. Brezing was sitting in a chair, according to Wurth, when Sarah threw an apple at him, causing his nose to bleed. One of the women then took his hat and put it on. They continued drinking until they were very drunk. Wurth went with the women to Mr. Heatherington's, where they got some more beer, and then to Sarah's house. Brezing did not return home that night, and Wurth and the two women stayed all night. Wurth stated that Sarah knew what room he stayed in with the other woman. She had come into the room, put on some men's clothing, and said she was going out. Wurth stayed until about an hour before daylight, when he left the woman there in bed. He had to leave early, he said, because it was market morning.

F. A. Sharp testified he had been in Mr. Cooke's Beer Saloon one night the previous winter when Sarah came in with another woman. She drank three or four glasses of beer, then took an apple out of her pocket and threw it at Brezing, smashing it on the wall over his head. According to Sharp, "She behaved herself very rudely"; and she said, "she was drunk as hell and didn't care who knew it," also that she was "not afraid of any Dutchman who ever lived." She then began to sing a song and dance a jig to it. Sharp further testified she ran up to Brezing, took him by the shoulder, shook him, and struck his head against the wall, causing his nose to bleed. She then took up a piece of the apple, wiped it in the blood on the floor, and, turning around, said, "Here is Dutchman's blood."

Cooke's saloon was on Mulberry (Limestone) Street between Main and Water Streets. Cooke was a German, whose true name was Philip Koch. His son would add a tragic chapter to Belle's life a few years later.

Samuel Coons, who signed his deposition with an "X (His Mark)," testified he had seen George Brezing drunk several times.

He also said he had, about a month earlier, seen him in a whorehouse about five o'clock in the evening and that he had stayed until about eleven that night.

John D. Millburn's deposition stated he had known George Brezing and his wife for nearly three years, and that he had seen Brezing in what he considered to be an intoxicated condition on several occasions. According to Millburn's testimony, Brezing would stay drunk sometimes for a week or two. His disposition when drunk, said Millburn, was generally boisterous. He had also heard Brezing and his wife quarreling several times within the previous two years. At one time in the store, Millburn saw Brezing hit his wife and knock her against the scales.

Thomas Webster testified he had seen Brezing drunk several times. On one occasion when Webster was working as a policeman, he and Officer Martin were approached by Mrs. Brezing and asked to go to her house because she said her husband had been whipping her. They went to the house but found it locked. (The girls were evidently locked inside with their drunken stepfather.)

Hester testified that she was thirteen years of age, that she was the daughter of Mrs. Brezing, and that she lived with her mother. She said she had seen her mother and Brezing quarreling and that she had seen Brezing

> . . . hit her [Sarah] with [his] fist. I have seen him hit her with a chair. I have seen him draw a knife on my mother. It was a butcher knife. I saw him draw a pistol on her. He would do these things when he was drunk. He broke some of the furniture in the house. . . . When he is drunk, his temper is bad.

On cross-examination, she said that Brezing was not her father.

Hester stated her mother had told Brezing she would burn the house, but added that her mother never threw matches or candles on the bed. (This must have been an answer to questions that were not recorded in the depositions.)

Brezing had been drunk, she said, about a week before the date of the deposition and had broken the showcase in the grocery store.

Belle was only six years old, too young to testify; but Hester gives evidence of the turmoil, fear, and mental anguish that surrounded the girls, the atmosphere that made them unacceptable to the mothers of children who would have been their natural playmates. "Their sins were visited on the children."

The divorce was granted to Sarah, and Brezing's counterclaim rejected. Brezing relocated to the northeast corner of Third and Henry Streets, where he opened yet another grocery/saloon and lived on the second floor of the establishment. This lasted less than a year, and he left town.

After the divorce, Sarah "took up" with William McMeekin, a

*This very revealing tintype shows Belle
when she was about eight years old. The
dress was probably much fancier than
other little girls might have worn.
Hardly visible are the dangling earrings
and the ring on her right index finger.
The flowers in her hair add to the
illusion of maturity. Both determination
and sadness are revealed in her face.*

local carriage painter, who was a few years her junior. There is no
evidence that the two ever married. They may have jumped over the
broomstick; but more likely, the jump was over the foot of the bed.
Sarah, however, changed the girls' surname to McMeekin and referred to herself as Mrs. McMeekin. She reported the family as such
to the census taker in 1870, when Belle was ten.

McMeekin was the son of William and Elizabeth McMeekin, residents of Lexington. The family had suffered an unusual tragedy
shortly before the younger William became involved with Sarah.

On a brisk evening in November of 1869, McMeekin's brother
Samuel had come home and, standing before the fire, was struck
down by a heart attack and died as he fell. When his mother was
informed, she, in turn, suffered a heart attack and died. The two
were buried in the Lexington Cemetery after a double funeral on
November 8, 1869. William's father had no talent or desire to keep
house and, a broken man, moved to a rooming house where he died
in a short time.

Thus, young William, dispossessed of a home and having no one,
was ripe for Sarah's picking. The match didn't last long, however;
and William moved out, leaving Sarah and the two girls alone once
more. Sarah thereafter listed herself as a seamstress and a widow.

When Hester reached sixteen, she took the first opportunity to get out and married John (Pick) Norton, a painter, on October 24, 1871, leaving Sarah and Belle, who was eleven, as the remainder of the ever-fluctuating family. Belle must have been lonely and vulnerable — at the mercy of anyone who showed her kindly attention.

At about this time, it was said, a man by the name of Dionesio Mucci "ruined" Belle. She was twelve years old. "Ruined" was the word used to describe a young girl's loss of virginity. It was recognized that she would no longer be acceptable as a wife; and it was assumed that now she would, for some reason, be eager to have sex again.

The Muccis came to Kentucky in 1864, seemingly after being in Ohio for a few years, since the 1870 census lists a son, Emile, who was eight and "born in Ohio." The Mucci family had all apparently lived in Gascony, Genoa, and Tuscany in Italy before coming to America.

Zachariah and Dionesio were brothers; and on February 13, 1867, a few months after their arrival in Lexington, they purchased a house and lot at Main and Georgetown Streets. Miss Neville said the Muccis "lived in the house facing on West Main, and the property elled around the corner with their hide, iron and paper business facing Georgetown Street." The business was known as Mucci & Bro.

According to the 1870 census, and judging from the order in which they were listed, there were Zachariah and his wife, Angeline; Dionesio and his wife Frederich (probably Fredericha), who was born in France. The latter two had sons Emile and Henry. There was also a Raphael Bonfantio, who boarded with the family.

Zachariah, who died in 1900, is listed in both censuses and city directories throughout his life in Kentucky as a musician. Dionesio ran the business and seemingly was a typical junk man of the time, driving a blind bay horse and wagon and, later, a two-horse spring wagon "painted drab color" around town, buying rags, paper, and scrap metal. In the course of business, he had several brushes with the law on charges of receiving stolen property. He purchased property in Brice's addition on South Mill Street, and part of the family lived there for a time.

Various deed, mortgage, census, and marriage records show unexplainable discrepancies regarding Dionesio's marriages. Although he apparently came to Kentucky with Frederich, he obtained a marriage license and married Mary Hack in 1868.

1868	Dionesio married Mary Hack (marriage record)
1870	Zachariah married to Angeline (census record)
	Dionesio married to Frederich (census record)
1875	Dionesio listed as "a single man" (mortgage record)
1880	Dionesio single
	Zachariah married to Angeline (deed record)

1881   Dionesio married to Angeline (deed record)
1887   Zachariah married to Angeline (deed record)

Dionesio and Zachariah are buried in Calvary Cemetery. Mary Hack, Frederich, and Angeline could not be found in any local cemetery; there is no record of a divorce.

Before Dionesio spoke to Belle, he must have watched her as she passed his house and hide yard only a short distance from her home. Perhaps it was her self-assurance that made her seem older than her years. Other children were always in groups, but this girl walked alone. There was a tilt to her head, a look on her face, a manner to her walk. It was all these things and something more. He couldn't identify it, but he thought of her more as a young woman than a child. He knew she was lonely, and he knew from the stories of her mother bringing home men that the little girl was wiser than her years.

It probably took little time for him to gain her confidence; and she would have done anything rather than give up this new friend, who was always glad to see her and never parted as he closed the store without first drawing her inside and kissing her goodby. Telling her to keep their hugs and kisses secret, this man in his thirties must have prompted a response from Belle; and he encouraged her defiance against the people who ignored her.

Belle realized in later years that she might have had a very different life had it not been for Mucci. She once told one of her "girls," Blanche Patterson, that she'd kill any man who ever took advantage of her daughter. Blanche said Belle was filled with emotion as she said it.

At the time, twelve was the legal age of consent in Kentucky; unless a girl was raped, the law took no action in the matter. If a girl had a father, or someone who cared, the guilty man was usually thrashed and run out of town, or killed. Of course, Belle had no father; and considering her mother's reputation, it is unlikely that anyone thought much of Belle's deflowering other than to remark that "the apple never falls far from the tree."

The liaison must have continued for some time; for it was on Valentine's Day in 1874, when Belle was fourteen, that she received her precious scrapbook inscribed,

> To Miss Belle Breezing Lexington, Ky.
> Presented by Mr. D. Mucci Feb. 14, 1874.

To a little girl who had already suffered from the ugliness of her home life and the rejection of her peers and even the community came the pain and stark realities usually reserved for a much older person. From the pleasure of having a real, grown-up friend to the eventual knowledge that she was being used. Too suddenly, the small body was forced to develop another layer to the exterior shell that hid the fear and loneliness and protected a tenderness she dared not let her world know was there.

Belle filled the scrapbook she got from Mucci with her personal treasures. In addition to Valentines (some German), there were birds from soda boxes, labels and premium pictures, magazine cutouts of ladies in the latest fashions, and myriad other items that caught her fancy.

Two early photographs from Belle's scrapbook. It is interesting to speculate if either could have been Sarah Brezing.

Undoubtedly Belle admired these illustrations of the latest fashions which she possibly clipped from Godey's Magazine or Peterson's Magazine.

There is no explanation of why these two black boys would appear in Belle's book.

It appears that there were only two children at this time who dared to be Belle's friends, Kate Parker and Willie Sutphin; and it is easy to imagine that Belle treasured the relationships. Kate's name appears several times in Belle's scrapbook. Willie, who was a year or so younger than Belle, wrote:

> I've often wished to have a friend,
> With whom my choice hours to spend,
> To whom I safely might impart,
> Each dream and weakness of my heart,
> And who would every sorrow hear,

And mingle with my grief a tear,
And to secure that bliss for life,
I'd wish for that friend to be my wife.

Yours truly,

Willie Sutphin

Though the poem was undoubtedly not his work, it must have appealed to the little boy as it surely did to Belle. For a child shunned by adults and children alike, it was wonderful to have a young admirer.

About the time Willie wrote of his devotion, Belle composed a poem of sorts for her book. It is a rambling dissertation that seldom rhymes. She titled it "Kisses."

Sitting to night in my chamber,
a school girl figure and lonely,
I kiss the end of my finger.
that and that only.
Reveries rises from the smokey mouth
Memories linger surround me.
Boys that are married or single.
Gather round me. School boys in pantalets roumping,
Boys that now are growing to be young lads,
Boys that like to be kissed, and like to give kisses.
Kisses—well I remember them;
Those in the corner were fleetest;
Sweet were those on the sly in the Dark were the sweetest
Girls are tender and gentle,
To woo was allmost to win them.
They lips are good as ripe peaches, and cream for finger.
Girls are sometimes flirts, and coquettish;
Now catch and kiss if you can sin;
Could I catch both—ah, wasn't I a happy Girl,
Boys is pretty and blooming sweetly, yea
Sweetness over their rest
Them I loved dearly and truely, Last and the best.

Writing by Belle Brezing, Lexington, Ky.

The author, obviously, was wise beyond her years, as she was just fourteen at the time. Belle's poem may have been only a dream; but others, hearing of Mucci's success, were doubtless making opportunities to get her alone.

Only a few months after Willie wrote in Belle's book, tragedy came. The young boy and a friend, George Sharp, were playing on Mill Street near Dudley School. They had a small pistol they thought to be a toy. Somehow it fired, and Sharp shot Willie just below the left eye. The bullet penetrated to the back of the skull. George dropped to his knees and beseeched his friend to get up, and assured him it was an accident. Willie's parents, who were out of town, were summoned. Two days later, on May 23, 1874, Willie died.

How dear a lost friend becomes. In later years, Belle must have thought often of that first love with someone her own age. Even if it was a childhood romance, it was sweeter than her memory of Mucci.

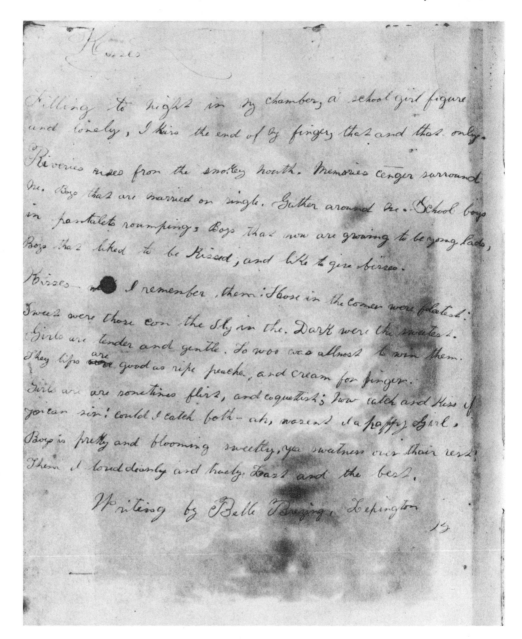

The original poem in Belle's handwriting, as it appears in the scrapbook, with its childish penmanship and misspellings.

CHAPTER 2

For Love – For Money

By the time Belle reached fourteen, her behavior was a growing source of gossip and amazement. Parents increased their guard against their children's contact with her. She was despised by the mothers, feared by the children, and used by the men. In rebellion, Belle tried to live up to her reputation.

Sarah may have been oblivious to her daughter's antics, or, more likely, didn't care. When most little girls wore discreetly plain little dresses, Sarah copied dresses from pictures Belle found in magazines and papers. As a result, the child was dressed in fashions suited to those far beyond her years. Sarah took darts in the bodices of Belle's dresses to better display her developing figure. After all, Sarah had no idea of what "virtue" meant.

Boys ready to step into manhood planned meetings with Belle on summer evenings in the cemetery out past her house, and she exchanged sex for what she thought was friendship and hoped would be love. The disappointment was almost overwhelming when a supposed new friend passed her the next day without speaking. The boys, involved in their first experience, found bragging to their friends about their adventure was almost as pleasurable as the act itself. The excitement grew with each telling; and the telling spread the word: The pretty little Brezing girl could be had.

Before her fifteenth birthday in 1875, Belle found she was pregnant. Seemingly still under the spell of Mucci, she had also taken up with a young boy by the name of Johnny Cook, who undoubtedly shared the sex she gave in exchange for attention. Johnny and his family had moved to Lexington from Nashville, Tennessee, where Johnny was born on August 24, 1859. After the death of his father (Philip Koch, who ran the saloon on Mulberry Street), his mother had remarried. The stepfather was Frederick Gobel, a German and also a saloonkeeper, whose establishment was at 9 Broadway, between Main and Short Streets, The Cooks were also German and had spelled their name "Koch" until after the father's death.

Belle and Sarah by this time had moved from West Short Street back to West Main, to a small house connected to the old grocery store on the corner of Georgetown Street, just past Mucci's junkyard.

Soon after Belle discovered her pregnancy, a series of events occurred that kept Lexington buzzing with gossip. On September 14, 1875, when she was three months pregnant, Belle married James Kenney, a nineteen-year-old boy who was apprenticed to "learn the art of cigar making" and who boarded on West Short Street. Kenney may have been with Belle on a summer night at the cemetery and perhaps was Sarah's choice of those who could be roped into a marriage. He had a job; and with a city ready to run her and her daughter out of town, marriage to anyone was the only hope she saw.

Kenney's mother signed the marriage bond as Katherine Kenny, along with Sarah, who used the name Sallie McMeekin. All signed with their "X" except Belle, the only one of the four who could read and write.

In a town where the newspaper usually took note only of marriages in "society," the press made an exception and used the opportunity to entertain their readers with little thought of the humiliation to Belle.

Lexington Daily Press
September 15, 1875

A marriage in high life is reported between Miss Belle Breezing and Mr. James Kinney. The ceremony was performed at the residence of the bride's mother. It was brief but most significant, and performed in a manner so touching that it drew tears from the eyes of those who witnessed it. La Belle Breezing is no more. She is now Mistress Kinney.

The tone of this article about a girl of fifteen certainly indicates that the newspaper knew this cruel sarcasm would chime in with the public's attitude.

Belle and James were married by the Justice of the Peace; and whatever the circumstances of the marriage, which are far from clear, Belle and Kenney did not live together. They may have shared a few nights; but if the boy did not then know he was being used, he was certain to have realized this following the events which occurred a few days later.

On September 23rd, just nine days after Belle's marriage, the new bride wrote Johnny Cook a note:

Lexington, Ky.

Dearest One. I will be down town at three o'clock look out for me. I will go to the office and by the store. Ma has come, have my pistol for me.

(She had given Cook a small derringer pistol that he had pawned. The pistol may have belonged to Sarah as the thought of the pistol and the report of her mother's return are in the same sentence.)

At four o'clock that day (an hour after Belle planned to meet him), Johnny Cook lay dead at her back gate, a bullet from the derringer lodged in his brain. Since the newspaper gave ample coverage, and it is our only source of information, we reprint here the reports of the *Daily Press* for September 24, 25, and 28, 1875.

LEXINGTON DAILY PRESS:

A SUICIDE OR A MURDER.

A Young Man is Found Dead, with a Pistol by His Side, in an Alley on Georgetown Street.

It is not often that it is the duty of a newspaper to report a more distressing occurrence than that which took place yesterday evening in this city. About four o'clock it was reported that a youth named John Cook, not more than seventeen years of age, was found dead in an alley on Jefferson street, between Main and Short. When the fact became generally known a curious throng gathered in the alley to view the remains of the unhappy boy, as he lay lifeless, his brain penetrated by a pistol shot, and by his side a small derringer, with which, apparently, the deed was done. He was well known and universally liked for his quiet, agreeable manners, and many were the expressions of regret from the bystanders at his untimely end, and of curiosity to learn the cause of the desperate act that terminated his young life.

Mr. Fritz Goebie, the step-father of the deceased, was upon the ground very soon, and at once took steps to make all necessary provision for the care of the dead. Esquire Charles Gibson being present, was requested by Mr. Goebel to act as coroner, which he did, impanneling a jury on the spot. The pockets of the deceased were searched, and there were found therein sixty cents in money, some cigars, and some notes addressed in lady's handwriting, but without date or name. They were as follows:

LEXINGTON, KY.
DEAR ONE:—Here it is and I want you to write to me when you go and believe me your truly girl as every, send me yours and don't forget it eather,
Your darling
BELLE.

LEXINGTON, KY.
DEAREST ONE:—I will be down town at three o'clock look out for me. I will go to the office and by the store. Ma has come, have my pistol for me.

These notes were addressed J. Cook, City.

Besides the notes was found a lock of hair and a photograph of a young woman, upon the back of which was written with pencil, "put this close to my heart."

The jury after brief consultation arrived at the following verdict:

"We, the jury, believe from the evidence before us, that the deceased, John Cook, came to his death by a shot from a pistol in his own hands."
CHAS. GIBSON,
Coroner.

During the examination by the jury, the poor afflicted mother of the youth appeared, and wrung all hearts by her piercing cries of anguish. She was gently removed from the dreadful scene and cared for by kind ladies present. But ever and anon she broke forth in wild lamentations for her poor boy. The scene was heartrending. The afflicted, grief-stricken mother was the object of intense sympathy and solicitude, the poignancy of her suffering bringing tears to the eyes of the beholders. It is not long since she lost by death a darling little daughter, and this second blow, so sudden and so startling, has prostrated the poor lady. Only mothers who have lost their loved ones by death can appreciate her distracted condition and fully sympathize with her in her heavy trial. Religion alone is able to offer her the consolation she so much stands in need of. May the holy angels bend her soul in resignation to the Divine Will. The Lord has given and the Lord hath taken away.

NOT ENDED YET.

And now truth compels the statement that there was no testimony offered before the jury that found the above verdict. No witness was examined and all the evidence that was considered was circumstantial. Very properly, the coroner, Mr. John Byrne, who was easily accessible, refused to recognize the jury verdict that had been rendered. He was on his way to the place where the man was killed when he met the remains being conveyed in a wagon to the home of the deceased. At this place the coroner impanneled another jury, took possession of the papers and adjourned the inquest until this morning at 9 o'clock. It may be useful to the jury to know that the young man had been in a good humor the whole day, that the notes he received and which were found on his person were received by him yesterday, and that to numerous friends he had expressed his intention of going to Cincinnati, all of which can be testified to by Mr. Strauss, with whom he was working, on Short street. It is useless to disguise a fact that is well known, that the young woman referred to in this sad affair, is Miss Belle Breezing, who married a few days ago a young man named Kinney, working in the same shop with Cook; that it was her picture the deceased had received that day; that he had met her as the notes intimated, and that he was seen walking home with her. About the time that he must have left her, or shortly after, at her residence on Main street, he entered the saloon of Mr. Garland, on Main street, and bought some cigars, treating a man who waited on him, to a cigar, and asking him to call on him in Cincinnati, whither he said he was going.

Within a few minutes afterwards, a Mr. Garland told a reporter of the PRESS, a colored man entered the store of Mr. Garland, and said that young Cook had shot himself in the alley. What evidence there was of this is not known. Certain it is that he lay at the back gate, opening into the yard where Belle Breezing lived, and that the gate was open when the jury gathered around the dead body. When the reporter of the PRESS saw him the pistol was lying upon his person; but it is said that when he was first seen the pistol was some distance from him. It is also stated that the same pistol was seen in a pawnbroker's shop, on Broadway, before the shooting.

More than this, persons who had talked with the deceased boy, represent him as saying that he was perfectly indifferent as to the fate or disposition of the young woman in question, creating the impression that he did not care whether she was married or not. Taking all this into consideration—the fact that he had stated to Mr. Strauss, where he worked, that he was going to Cincinnati, his good humor during the day, the joking that he had withstood from Mr. Strauss in regard to the marriage and the express statement at Mr. Garland's store that he was going to Cincinnati, it is difficult to believe that the unfortunate young man committed suicide. The wound is above the temple and is a long one, over an inch, and in the absence of any other testimony it is possible that the shot was accidental or worse.

At any rate the coroner's jury which meets at nine o'clock this morning, should have before it every possible material witness, and if any foul play has been perpetrated it should, if possible be brought to light. The boy Kinney who married Belle Breezing was a fellow worker with Cook, but what his doings were during the day, our reporter so far, has not been able to ascertain. It is in no idle spirit of news gathering that these words are written but with the hope that the truth may be discovered and that this tangled skein may be unravelled.

POST MORTEM AFFECTION.

Belle Brezing Indites a Rhyming Obituary to her Dead Lover.

Heaven, from a Worldly Point of View.

Miss Belle Brezing, the heroine of one of the most unfortunate tradegies that have ever shocked the people of this community, a woman whom it has been the fashion to publicly call by her christian name, sends for publication in the PRESS, a poem expressive of her feelings in regard to the young man who "killed hisself." As Miss Belle is apt to say what she means, and mean what she says, just as much now as before she became Mistress Kinney, it may be truthfully said of the beautiful thoughts in the verse which we have the honor to publish under her signature, that " them's her sentiments." It is stated on reliable authority, and henceforth will be regardded as the very essence of the truth of history, that La Belle went to the house where her deceased "friend" lay dead, and made her way to the presence of the corpse under the eyes of the agonized mother, under the impression, perhaps, that the inquest was to be held there, or may be to mingle her salt lake oozings with the scalding tears that came of maternal anguish. It is recorded that she did not stay there long. The place was unhealthy for her, the maternal feelings were too strong and the mother's instinct too expressive as to the cause of her boy's death. If the corruption may be allowed,

Lady Clara Vere de Vere
Heard what wasn't nice to hear.

Miss Belle left in a hurry, reserving her smooth emotion for a post obit rhyme, which is given below, and which, of course, was prepared upon the spur of the moment and under the inspiration of one who was acquainted with the geography of the next world. The sentiments which it expresses are chaste and beautiful, betraying such intimacy with things heavenly as will surprise those who do not know this gifted young person, or who have been in the habit of associating her with the most mundane of sublunary pastimes. Henceforth let scoffers be silenced, and let no man doubt the claims of La Belle Brezing as heir-at-law to the mansions in the skies and the confidential friend of the ferryman of the Styx.

In reading over the rhythmical sentimentality which follows, let all true loviers place their hands upon their hearts, and, with bowed heads exclaim, here is love without guile.

To the editor, Miss Belle, in the anguish of her spirit, addresses the following note:

Please put this in the Press and Dispatch if want pay, send me word oblige Belle Brezing.

Of course, under the circumstauces, it is with melancholy pleasure we print the following graveyard rhyme:

JOHNNIE COOK—GONE TO HIS REST.
[Written and composed by BELLE BREZING, Lexington, Ky.]

His busy hands are folded,
  His work on earth is done;
His trials all are ended,
  His heavenly crown is won.

Upon his brow so peaceful
  No earthly shadows rest ;
For anxious cares reach never
  The mansions of the blest

Within the home he brightened
  His quiet course has run—
A life of pure unselfishness—
  A man's work well done.

No titles high and sounding,
  Shed such a holy light
As crowns that brow so faded,
  Now passed from earthly blight.

The sad and lonely household
  Will miss his guiding hand ;
The daughters, loving, clinging,
  Without his aid must stand.

The childen, mother's counsel
  Will seek, on earth, no more:
No more hishand will lead them,
  Save on the heavenly shore.

The flowers he loved and tended
  Are nipped by wintry frost ;
His life with theirs departed,
  O'ershadowed, but not lost.

For in the Spring time coming
  They'll burst the prison bond ;
So, too, that form, now lifeless,
  Will rise to life beyond.

There on the shores eternal,
  His spirit beckoning stands,
Still guiding on his loved ones
  To join the heavenly bands.

SEPT. 24th, 1875.

The paper had again taken the opportunity to ridicule Belle, whose poem, with its references to children, etc., obviously was not written about this young boy of eighteen.

SUICIDE OR MURDER.

A Case for the Grand Jury.

There is a prevailing sentiment in this community that the young man John Koch, who was found dead in an alley, between Main and Short, on Thursday evening last, did not kill himself, although that is the opinion of two Coroner's juries. There is evidence that is most important which has not been before the jury at all. A gentleman, a professor of language, met the unfortunate youth but a moment or two before his death, after he left Garland's grocery, and reports that he was perfectly sober and in his usual good humor. Another declares that he was upon the ground a moment after the shooting, and saw a man in the gateway leading to the Breezing residence, and which Belle Brezing swore was nailed up. Another witness declares that he was there still earlier and that the body was lying partly inside the gateway so declared to be nailed up. When first seen by young Hord the pistol was some distance from the dead body, four or five feet, in a moment or so afterwards it was lying upon his breast. Who had taken the pains to put it there? Why was not the mother of the girl examined? Was she not in the house? Why was not Belle Brezing forced to tell who was in the house at the time of the killing? Why did young Koch come away from Belle Brezing's house without giving up the pistol as he had intended, in answer to the request contained in Belle Brezing's note? When he sent for her to come into the alley did he not expect she would go the back way, and did he not intend to give up the pistol? Who was the negro Koch was in conversation with outside of Garland's grocery, and was he not, perhaps, proposing to him to take back the pistol for him? Is it not likely he wanted to deliver the pistol to the owner in the alley? From the time that young Koch left Mucci's, where he was last seen, until he reached the gate where he died, not more than two minutes could have elapsed. Did he decide on suicide in that brief time? Did he have his clothes cleaned in order that he might commit suicide? A gentleman in this city, whose name will not be mentioned unless the case comes before the grand jury, believes, from a remark which he overheard a night or two before, that it was not a suicide; but he will not state what he heard. Is not this a case for the consideration of the grand jury? Does it not appear that the evidence upon which the coroner's jury brought in a verdict of suicide, is mighty slim? The truth is, there is a wide-spread belief in this city that there has been foul play in the treatment of the dead youth, and the public sentiment will not be satisfied until there is a more thorough and searching investigation.

James Kenney, Belle's husband of nine days, disappeared either before or just after the shooting. It appears strange that Mucci was the last person to see Johnny alive. The paper asks why Sarah was not questioned and insinuates that Belle was lying about the gate being nailed. The question is also raised as to who was in the house. The event is certainly replete with suspects. We don't know what Sarah's feelings were toward the boy or, for that matter, what went on between Johnny and Belle in that hour between three and four.

Mucci, if he thought Johnny was the father-to-be, might have shown a deep jealousy. He was the last one to see the boy alive, and the death scene was only a few feet from his place of business. Certainly the prime suspect was James Kenney. What were the circumstances surrounding his leaving town?

He returned to Lexington in 1887 after an absence of over ten years. He worked as a cigar maker for John Weigart on East Fifth Street for about a year, then left town again, returning the second time around 1894. He died in Lexington on August 22, 1915. If he ever saw his wife Belle again, it was only in passing on the street.

Johnny Cook and James Kenney are buried in the Lexington Cemetery; Mucci, Sarah, and Belle lie just across the street in Calvary (the Catholic cemetery). The answers to the mysteries surrounding the events of September 23, 1875, are buried with them.

On March 14, 1876, Belle was delivered of a little girl she named Daisy May Kenney. If there was joy at the birth, it was short-lived; two months later, on May 17th, Belle's mother died.

Sarah was laid to rest on a rainy day in a single grave lot in Calvary Cemetery, only a few blocks from where she had lived. Although the section she was buried in was not called "potter's field," the single grave lots were the place where the poor were interred.

There were few who cared enough to go to the graveside services in the rain. Hester was there with John Norton. They then lived at the corner of Cox Street and the railroad, a block from where Belle and her mother were residing at the time of Sarah's death and scarcely more than a block from the cemetery. Belle was there, holding Daisy May and covering her against the rain. Mrs. Barnett, a neighbor who lived across the street on West Main, being a woman of kindness, had come for Belle's sake. She knew Belle's story; and although she did not approve, she certainly had seen Sarah enough to know that the girl had had little chance to be different. She also knew Mucci; and after she heard what he had done to Belle, she turned her head when he passed her house. Together with the priest who intoned the short service, these few made up the mourners as Sarah was lowered into the grave.

When it was over, Belle, with Daisy May cradled in her arms, walked slowly back to town with Mrs. Barnett beside her as a gentle spring rain fell. As they came up the hill from the railroad tracks, Belle saw what must have made her heart sink. The landlord, irate because no rent had been paid since Sarah became ill, had taken the opportunity afforded by the funeral and Belle's absence to move all the furniture out on the street and padlock the house. The two women walked to the pitiful pile of belongings and stood for a moment and watched the water soak the mattresses and clothes.

Mrs. Barnett must have felt a great deal of sympathy for this teenager standing with her child in what was now a downpour, for she displayed more courage in showing her kindness than anyone else in town would have. John Norton could understandably have not wanted his wife to have anything to do with Belle, and there is no record of their ever having any association during his lifetime. Although the girls had clung to each other as children, it was different now. Hester had always been timid and now wanted a new life. Her mother was gone, and she would not let Belle and her reputation come between her and her husband.

Mrs. Barnett agreed to take the baby home with her; and Belle placed the child in the older woman's arms, asking if she would keep her "just till I find a place to live." And she promised to pay for Daisy's keep. Mrs. Barnett's only stipulation was that Belle not come to the house when her sons Lou and Asa were at home. Belle understood this and agreed without further comment.

As the woman hurried across the street to put dry things on the baby, Belle picked up a few pieces of clothing, some pictures, and her scrapbook and tied them in an old quilt. Turning, she started walking away. Mrs. Barnett, busy with the baby, did not see where she went.

She could have gone a few doors to Mucci's; and if he was not then married (to one of the three women who so mysteriously passed through his life as wives), he might have taken her in. Somewhere she found shelter for the night. Perhaps she traded herself; after all, her body was all she had.

It is uncertain what Belle did and where she lived for the next two years. In an interview years later, Mrs. Margaret Egbert, Lexington's first policewoman, who had known Belle since childhood, said the girl lived for a time on South Mill Street between High and Maxwell and had a boyfriend who was a known counterfeiter. The only concrete evidence we have of Belle's residence is contained in the 1877–78 City Directory, which lists Belle as living on Jefferson Street, near Short; no man's name is associated with the listing.

Whatever her life was, it is not likely that it was an easy one. For an "unchaste" woman with Belle's reputation could be used, but could never become a wife or homemaker unless she was ready to accept the abuse of a man who would periodically resent her past life and be revolted at the thought that he had, in a rash moment, made such a mistake as to marry her. In the Victorian era, there was only good and evil, black and white; no gray area existed. Going back and starting over was not allowed.

A woman in such a position was frequently passed from hand to hand, given small amounts of money and bedded until the novelty wore off. Then one morning, the man was gone; and the girl was left to find another to be "good to her." It was a state of semi-prostitution; and as the men stayed with her for shorter periods and new lovers were more frequent, she was moved to a state that can only be described as prostitution.

It was hard to live as she did. Too often the boys and men did not understand that their gifts of money were her only means of living. They did not seem to know they were going to bed with a girl who required material support. It was hard to ask in advance when the man, usually someone she knew, approached the whole affair as though it were a meeting of lovers. Every man and boy had talked to another who had slept with her, and her reputation was such that they thought she wanted them. She had never been able to admit, even to herself, that she was a prostitute. She felt as though these men would want to give her money if she was good to them. Always she thought she would find someone who would love her and make a home for her and Daisy May. Now, anything was better than the way she lived. A bawdy house was all that was left.

At a house, the madam collected the money as though it was her charge for the use of the room, or as though she was selling the girl without even consulting her. On the way to the room, the girl could make some snide remark about the older woman that would somehow set her apart from the commercial part of the transaction. "That old bitch always wants her money." It definitely made a difference whose hand the money was placed in.

It would be better to be in a house like the new one Jennie Hill had opened than to worry about where the next meal would come from, how she would have the money for Mrs. Barnett on Saturday, or to live with the constant fear that the landlord would evict her.

These thoughts had formed over days of worry; and on December 24, 1879, when Belle found herself alone and without money, her rent long overdue, as well as the money for Daisy May's board, her options narrowed to one. Loneliness intensifies at Christmas time. There was no heat in her room, and she had already borrowed from everyone within the distance she could carry a bucket of coal. She had found that most women would give her coal just to get her off their stoop. Her mind was made up by the circumstances, not by her. Given this situation, it is easy to imagine what Belle's next steps would be.

In the cold room, she slipped off her clothes and hurriedly put on her best dress. It was the last one her mother had made for her, and she always kept it for special. Putting on her coat and wishing she had gloves, she turned and looked at the dismal room. As the lamp flickered for the want of oil, she picked up her scrapbook and walked out. If the landlord did not lock up her few possessions for back rent, she could get them later. If her plan worked and she could get an advance of money, she did not care what happened to the things.

It had been snowing all day, and the lamplighter had not passed yet. She had trouble on the uncleaned walks. At the corner she turned to look at the Barnetts' house. She knew the woman would see that Daisy had a nice Christmas. There would be fruit and candy and all the food that went with the excitement of the holidays. How wonderful it would be to spend the night there and wake up the next morning with Daisy beside her, the house warm and filled with the smell of a roasting bird. But that could not be; and she hurried on, her thin coat pulled close around her as she clutched the scrapbook to her breast. No one was on the street, and she was glad. If a man had come up and asked her to go back to the room, she might have tried again, so great was her fear of what lay ahead.

When she pulled the bell at Jennie Hill's big house on Main Street, seconds seemed like minutes. She thought she would freeze as she waited for someone to answer.

A colored girl came to the door and was surprised to see a woman. Belle asked if Miss Jennie was in. The girl said, "Yes," and was about to close the door, never having been told what to do if it were not a man wanting in; but Belle hurriedly stepped inside. She had never been in such a fine house, and she tried to see it all at one glance so that she could remember in case she was rejected. She looked at the mirrors and pictures on the walls and what furniture she could see. She could hear people talking in the room to her right, and a man laughed in another room further down the hall. Staying close to the front door so she could not be seen from the rooms, she removed her coat, though still freezing, knowing her dress made a better appearance, and stood waiting until the girl returned with Jennie.

The older woman recognized her from seeing her on the street, although they had never spoken. After all, Belle's reputation was equal to Jennie Hill's, even if she did not have a house.

The madam said very flatly, "What do you want?" Belle could have cried, not only for her fear of the woman, but for all the past and the unknown future.

"Can I board here?" she asked. When there was no immediate reply, she added, "Be one of your girls."

Jennie continued to look at her. Then she turned and looked at the servant girl, who immediately retreated down the hall and out of sight. Turning again to Belle, she asked, "What about that baby of yours?"

"I've got her boarding up the street. She won't be around."

"You ain't sick, are you? I don't want no girls with disease."

"No," Belle said. "I never had anything."

The older woman seemed to soften slightly. "I got rules. They got to be followed, and I get half."

"Yes, ma'am." Belle had never been humble, but now so much depended on her acceptance.

"You got to be nice to the men and do what they want."

"Yes, ma'am."

"I don't allow no fighting among my girls. You got to get along."

"Yes, ma'am. I won't cause trouble."

"Well, I guess we can try it, but I don't like town girls too much in my house."

Belle didn't answer.

"Have you had anything to eat?"

"No, ma'am." Belle decided not to ask about an advance or to mention that she had no clothes fit to wear. That could wait until to-morrow.

Without raising her voice, Jennie said, "Amanda," and the black girl reappeared. "Take her upstairs to the last room in the back, light the grate, and take her up something to eat." Turning to Belle, she said, "You want to start tonight? We got a lot of men coming in."

Belle couldn't sort out her emotions. She was thankful to be in out of the cold, and she was glad she was going to get something to eat, but there was too much in a new life and too much in an old life to know where the tears were coming from that she held back with so much effort. "Could I wait until tomorrow night?"

"All right," Jennie replied. "Go on up, and we'll talk in the morning."

And so it was on Christmas Eve, 1879, at the age of nineteen, that Belle Brezing became one of Jennie Hill's girls and spent the first night in the big house where Abraham Lincoln had visited his wife's

The Mary Todd Lincoln House has been restored and is on the National Register of Historic Places. The grocery store was built into the house some time after Jennie Hill's occupancy.

family in 1847 and 1850.

She was afraid she would not sleep. She heard the bells at St. Paul's and thought the midnight mass was about to start. She had stopped going to church, but there was always that worry that hung over her. As the room warmed and she pulled the covers up about her, she heard men's voices in the hall and a girl laughed in the next room. But soon all the troubles somehow faded, and she slept the deep sleep said to be reserved for the innocent.

She woke early and lay in bed because she heard no sounds. The fire had died out, and she thought how cold it would be when she got up. Finally, she could wait no longer. She wanted to see the rest of the house, and she was hungry. She had slept in her slip; and she put her other clothes on, shivering in the cold. It was Christmas morning, she thought. Before she let her mind drift, she said, almost aloud, "Things could be worse."

Quietly, she opened the door and went out into the hall. Downstairs, she found three sitting rooms, all filled with furniture she thought very fine. All the fires had been banked the night before, and even her excitement at getting a better look at the mirrors and pictures and the big chairs and couches could not stop her chills.

At the end of the hall, she found a door she thought would be the kitchen and, opening it, felt the warm air. Amanda, who had answered the door the night before, had her back to the room and was working at the stove. When she turned, if she was startled to see Belle standing there, she didn't act so. "Merry Christmas," she said. "What you doin' up so early? You want somethin' to eat?"

"Merry Christmas," Belle replied. "Yes, I'm hungry."

Belle sat at the big round table as the girl worked about the stove. From the warmer, she took ham that she had fried earlier. She opened the oven and brought out hot biscuits; then moving a lid on the stove, she began to fry eggs. "I'm fixin' the food and settin' it aside. Miss Jennie say I could go home and be with my folks till time for business tonight."

Soon Belle felt much better, but she found out little about the house from the girl, who evidently preferred that Jennie tell this stranger what she wanted to know and who was obviously in a hurry to go home for Christmas.

The house which Jennie Hill rented was owned during the time of her occupancy by Selby Lilliston.

Jennie was a rather tall, angular woman, as may be judged by her photograph. Her "house" was the finest in town, and she was well-known in the city and to many men who had occasion to visit Lexington and sought such mundane pleasures as are offered in a bawdy house. Garland Hale, a traveling minstrel who played the old Opera House at Main and Broadway, would sing:

> I am an esthetic young man.
> My name is Jim McCann.
> I pay all the bills at Jennie Hill's.
> So tra la, la, la, young man.

It must have been a show-stopper, for it was long remembered and often repeated in later years by old gentlemen who had heard Hale.

The 1880 census, taken six months after Belle's arrival at Jennie Hill's, showed the following to be occupants of the house:

Jennie Hill	white	female	33	single	housekeeper
Mag Lyons	"	"	18	"	boarder
Belle Brezing	"	"	19	"	"
Maude Jones	"	"	24	"	"
Dolly Morgan	"	"	20	"	"
Lue Bennett	"	"	43	"	"
Ann Bishop	"	"	25	"	"
Amanda Johnson	black	"	17	"	servant

Belle was liked by the other girls at Jennie's, but that was only because she made consistent efforts to talk with them and always seemed interested in what they had to say. Were it not for this exceptional effort, the other girls would have hated her. She was always the first to be selected when men came to the house and the girls were called to the front parlor. It took a great deal of diplomacy on Belle's part to mollify a girl who lost one of her "regulars" to her.

Belle never bragged about the large tips she received, knowing she far outdistanced everyone in the house. Other than the purchase of necessary clothes and the amount she paid to Mrs. Barnett for

LEXINGTON, KY.

Studio picture of Jennie Hill, madam of the first house Belle worked in as a prostitute. The gaudy dress is a distinct contrast to the finer gowns later worn by Belle.

keeping Daisy May, she was miserly in her spending. From the first month at Jennie's, Belle had planned to stay only as long as it would take to save the money to strike out on her own. If this was to be her lot, she would be "the highest class whore this town's ever seen."

Every contact with anyone of importance commanded her total attention. Bankers promised — secretly, of course — to advise her in financial matters, often without the knowledge that their sons, young men who were "coming up" in the bank, had made similar promises as she lay in their arms in the big feather bed.

Politicians, especially the young ones who were "going places," found pleasures with Belle. They certainly had her undivided attention and affectionate behavior they never dreamed existed.

She cleverly suggested an arrangement with her important clients whereby they could send her a note by a servant or messenger, and she would be at the back door off Merino, the dark side street, at an appointed time to let them in. This prevented their being seen at the front door, which opened right onto Main Street. Thus, they were assured privacy, something Jennie and the other girls never thought of.

She learned not only what men were like, but also the differences there were in men that made them all so much alike. She caught their words and phrases. The inflections in their voices. She had no women to study, but she could pick out the boys who were raised alone by mothers and adoring aunts. They had more feminine thoughts. They spoke as they heard the women talk, and she learned from them.

In a time when even many married men had not seen a nude woman (it was considered indecent for a wife to disrobe in the presence of her husband and the conjugal act was performed in total darkness), Belle made hearts pound as she slowly disrobed. Although her talk was quite salty, she measured her words and never appeared crude to her ever-increasing clientele of the rich, the important, and the influential.

Prostitution has existed in Kentucky since pioneer days, and there are several references to this institution prior to 1800, but it was Belle Brezing who raised it to an art form.

In a few weeks, she had outgrown Jennie Hill's and saw the flaws in the operation. It was disconcerting to the madam when she heard that a visit to her house was often referred to as "going up to Belle's." The young girl made money for Jennie, but Belle made more for herself and certainly saved more.

Finally, on July 1, 1881, after she had been with Jennie a year and a half, she began to set the wheels in motion to open her own house.

The row house, presently designated as 314–316–318 North Upper Street, where Belle opened her first house.

CHAPTER 3

Madam Belle

Belle rented a portion of a row house on North Upper Street across from the Transylvania College campus. (There were already other "houses" in the area and on the same street.) With a small down payment, she acquired rugs, drapes, and curtain material from Brown & Scott Co. How she was able to obtain a mortgage for the balance due on her purchases is not clear, but a mortgage is recorded in the Fayette County Courthouse. She certainly had none of the usual assets required by lenders; but then again, she had other assets that may have been well-known to the merchants she was dealing with.

Her first large purchase was on July 8, 1881, and consisted of:

147 yards of Brussels carpet [Carpeting came in strips and was sewed together to make the desired size rug.]
80 yards of Ingrain carpet
2 cornice poles
7 cornices
160 yards of lining [for drapes]
1½ dozen stair rods
1½ dozen stair pads
2 Brussels rugs
3 pairs of curtains
32 yards of muslin curtains [drapes]
10 red shades and fixtures [oil lamps]

Belle set right to work; and with the sewing she had learned from Sarah and the help she was able to hire, she began making drapes and curtains and had the carpets laid. (The stair rods and pads indicate she had possession of more than one unit in the two-story row building, which still stands.)

Three days later, on July 11th, Belle was ready for the furniture and went to town to get it. She again required a sizable mortgage, which is on record at the Fayette County Courthouse, for the following:

1 fine French dresser suit of furniture
Another like suit of furniture
3 dressing case suits of furniture
1 parlor suit of furniture
1 pier glass
A dozen chairs
One-half dozen chairs
3 wardrobes
1 sofa
1 eight-foot table
4 mattresses
5 sets of springs
1 portable set of springs
1 pair of sham pillows
6 bolsters

Judging from the five bedroom suits, she planned for four girls and herself.

Evidently, she paid cash for the other household necessities and the bric-a-brac she loved.

The pleasurable excitement of setting up her own house was lost in the discovery that Daisy May was retarded. Both the doctor and Mrs. Barnett had known for some time that the child was not normal, but Belle would not believe it. She went several times a week to see Daisy May and always left in tears. Finally, Mrs. Barnett could no longer handle the little girl; she forced Belle to see that something must be done. The doctor advised that the child be sent to the asylum on Fourth Street, but Belle would have none of it. Finally, from the church, she found out about a school and institution run by nuns in Newport, Kentucky, where Daisy would be taught what she was capable of learning. And so, when she was about six years old, Daisy May was sent to live in northern Kentucky in the school where Belle was assured she would have love and care and be with other children her age. She was enrolled under the name of Daisy Barnett. Since Belle was widely known by then, it is quite possible Mrs. Barnett took the child to Newport and used her own name to avoid any connection with Belle.

Mrs. Barnett and the doctor were the only ones other than Belle who knew where Daisy May went. A story of Belle's choice was leaked to explain Daisy May's departure. "Belle Brezing's girl is in an expensive girls' school in the East."

Her first arrest came in 1882. She realized there were forces that would some day put her out of business. Every raid, every fight, every killing was ammunition for the people who would one day close the houses of prostitution in Lexington. Belle knew there would be prostitution till the end of time; and she thought girls in houses, in designated areas, was the way it should be. But all the meetings of concerned citizens, all the sermons, and all the political speeches said otherwise. Belle was never requested to give an opposing view. She was the town's best authority, but was never asked for her opinion.

One of the more interesting items in the expanded Brezing collection is a small, red, leather-bound journal which was one of Belle's first account books and covers the years 1882 and 1883.

In the journal, each girl is listed and daily records kept of her earnings. The names (in their original spellings) are Blanch Johnson, Mattie Waid, Maud Surville, Ena Livingston, Matie Stone, Nettie Denhart, Ethal Maguirer, Gussie Graves, Mamie Clayton, Edna Martin, Frankie Wright, Belle Dennis, Daisy Brooks, Jesie Roe, Frankie Hill, Matie Courtney, Lillie Kahn, Lillie Bell, Ida Grant, Lida Stone, Effie Howard, Sue Downing, Ruby Veit, Mina Sayer, and Lottie Brown.

Twenty-five girls over the two years covered by the journal, if we are to believe each name was a different girl. Most, if not all, were assumed names; and the girls were free to change them if they found one they liked better.

In almost all cases, each girl made $16.00 and then quit for the week, as indicated by the journal. Or perhaps, after the girls satisfied their obligation to the house at $16.00, their other earnings were not a matter with which the madam was concerned. The entries usually began on Monday; if their earnings totaled $16.00 by Tuesday, there are no entries under their names until the following Monday. Some girls made as much as $13.00 in one night, and a few went over the usual amount and made as much as $20.00 in a week.

Seemingly, it was a dollar house, as there are several entries for this amount. Belle later elevated her place to a $5.00 house, but even $1.00 was a good amount in a time when men's wages for labor were 50¢ to a $1.00 a day. Few jobs were open to women at that time, and female clerks were fortunate to get work at 10¢ an hour and frequently worked sixty-hour weeks. The old expression was, "You can make more on your back than you can standing on your feet."

The book includes day-to-day accounts of the operation. There are grocery lists, laundry lists, horse boarding payments, phaeton storage costs, and payments marked "to board" at $20.00 a week. This may have been the amount Belle paid to Mrs. Barnett, who probably took care of Daisy May's tuition, a further indication that Belle did not want to run the risk of causing Daisy May to suffer the same prejudice she had endured because of Sarah. Mrs. Barnett is mentioned in another section of the journal by name. Several times, the amount beside her name is less than $20.00, but there is no indication what she was being paid for.

The earnings of several of the "inmates" or "girls" are marked "paid to Jim," with no explanation.

Every trip to the grocery included the purchase of vinegar (from the amount purchased, it was undoubtedly used for purposes other than cooking), and coal oil for lamps was purchased daily as it was considered dangerous to keep too much of the highly inflammable material on hand. Bread 5¢. Meat 20¢. Milk 10¢. Bird seed 10¢ (Belle, in keeping with the tradition of whorehouses, had a parrot). Meal and flour 10¢. For picnic $1.00. There is a $2.00 charge to coal (probably a ton). There are several purchases of cigarettes.

Other interesting entries include:

Blanch Johnson's account was charged with: trunk $32.25, dress
    $11.00, dress $5.50, medicine $2.00, beer $1.00
Milk bill $14.70 (for what period is not shown)
Work $50.00
White work $5.00
Phaeton to Paris $2.50
Board Archie 75¢
My expenses for the first week in January $48.20

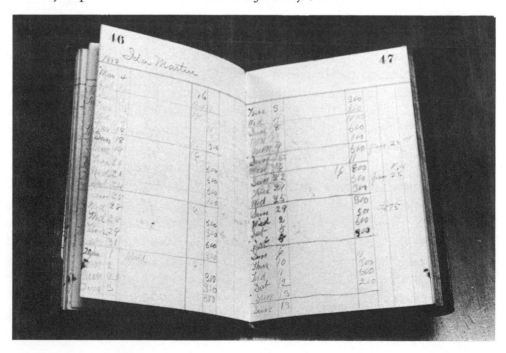

Pages in the little red journal in which Belle kept her records 1882–1883.

Belle must have done well right from the start. As time would prove, she was a clever businesswoman. She quickly paid off the mortgages on the furniture and acquired more without a mortgage. But tragedy struck again. She found she was pregnant only a few months after she opened her own house.

Although male contraceptives had been available for some time, they were not popular with the men and were seldom used except by those fearful of contracting a venereal disease. Other girls would have performed their own abortions, or acquired the help of one of the women available for a fee. But Belle was conscious of her Catholic commitment, and abortion was out of the question. Usually, it was the lazy girls who didn't get up and take care of themselves at once who found themselves in this condition. The only protection they had was vinegar, then used as a spermatocide, as well as a germicide.

The pregnancy must have been devastating to Belle, who was soon reduced to sitting behind a table in the parlor so that her condition would not show and collecting the money as the girls carried on the business.

On the night that Belle felt the first pain, the house was closed, the downstairs lights turned off to discourage visitors, and the doctor sent for. It was an exceptionally warm night, and the delivery had complications. The curtains did not stir at the open window. The girls sat in the darkened rooms and spoke in hushed tones. Belle suffered as she had never suffered before. It was in that quiet time just before dawn that the baby finally came, but there was no cry to break the stillness of the deserted street. The child was stillborn.

Belle was in no condition to help with the necessary arrangements. The girls and the doctor prepared for the burial as Belle drifted in and out of consciousness. She would have wanted the baby buried in Calvary Cemetery; but since the child had been born to a prostitute, the girls feared to approach the church. The burial was in Lexington Cemetery, where the record card reads:

> July 13, 1882
> Brezin, Belle, infant
> Section G-1 Lot 121
> Grave 48   Burial #7830

This is a single grave lot, and once again the misspelling of Brezing appears.

Belle lay for some days, taking only the least nourishment; and it was feared she would die. But once more she called on all the strength she could muster from her small body. In a few weeks, she was back managing the house, watching the girls, and planning to expand her operation beyond what her present quarters would allow.

It was in December of 1882 that pressure was brought on the police, and Belle was arrested on the charge of "operating a bawdy house" and her case held to the grand jury. She was released on bond (which was posted in cash). Many were delighted at the arrest and could hardly wait for her to be tried and convicted. Actually, she had already been convicted by her enemies; the trial was only a formality. However, they had not allowed for the connections Belle had made. The local court received the following instrument of pardon from the governor of the state.

With the pardon, Belle found great enjoyment in going out to be seen by the townspeople. Beautifully attired as always, her head held high, looking straight ahead, she saw from the corner of her eye the open mouths and gawking stares of people who hated her even more now that she had been sprung from the trap. The satisfaction was doubled when she saw someone whose scorn or cutting words had broken her heart as a child.

She owned a handsome, high-spirited, chestnut stallion; and she rode it sidesaddle in the manner of the time. Always in an exquisite riding habit, she knew she was sending blood pressures soaring. In some of the men, it was desire; in women, it was hatred.

On May Day, 1883, as she rode down Main Street amidst the crowds celebrating the holiday, two small boys, excited by their holiday play, startled her horse. It bolted and fell, rolling over on her. She sustained a severe blow to her head and lay unconscious for hours. The doctor feared the blow might result in "brain fever" and death. The women of the town, along with a small account in the newspaper, spread the word: At last, Belle Brezing had gotten what she had coming.

Men who witnessed the accident marveled that she was not unseated when the horse first bolted. (They admired good horsemanship.) They were certain she would have "stayed up" had the animal not fallen.

Once more, Belle's determination carried her through what would have been a long recuperation for a "shrinking violet"; and she was up and in control of her house a few nights later.

Not wanting to give the town the satisfaction of seeing her fall again (and perhaps because of a fear she wouldn't admit), she bought the finest phaeton to be had, with a matched team of chestnuts, whose coats glistened in the sunlight, and continued her outings in even grander style. With a liveried Negro driver in a tall, black hat, she was frequently seen about town, dressed in the highest fashion. She was aware that the whole town talked about her; and, of course, these excursions were the best form of advertising available to her.

Belle was indicted again, in 1883; she was tried in absentia, and the fine was paid by her attorney.

On July 18, 1883, Belle purchased from Alice and J. R. Jackson a house, just up the street from where she was living, at 194 North Upper Street (near the corner of Fourth Street; this was the address at the time of the purchase before the numbers were changed).

The newspaper usually gave scant attention to the funeral of a prostitute, and some deaths were completely ignored. It was evidently a slow day for news in 1882 when the paper devoted considerable space to the funeral of one of Jennie Hill's girls. Doubtless, a

Belle standing at the front gate of 194 North Upper Street with her girls and servants. The wreath on the door must indicate a death, possibly Rebecca Hall, who was buried in Belle's lot in 1887. The picture was torn when discarded after Belle's death.

wreath such as that shown in the preceding photograph hung on the front door of Jennie's house in memory of Fannie.

At Rest.

The last sad rites of burial were given the remains of Mrs. Fannie Parshall, *nee* Fannie Davis, at 4 o'clock last Saturday afternoon. Her death occurred in this city on Friday, March 10th, at the residence of Miss Jennie Hill, on Main street, and was caused from softening of the brain. Her maiden name was Fannie Brandenberg, and her home, prior to her. marriage to Mr. Parshall, an express agent on the Lexington & Cincinnati Railroad, was in Clarksville, O. She was finely educated, having graduated from the Ladies' Female Seminary, at Hillsboro, O. The services were conducted by by Rev. Dr. Bartlett, of the First Presbyterian Church, and were very sad and impressive. His remarks to her friends will long be cherished in their memories, and his assurance that the Lord had said, "Him that cometh unto Me shall in nowise be cast out," will forever be a source of great consolation to them. Her grave, in the Lexington Cemetery, was beautifully decorated with flowers. At the head was a broken floral column, surmounted by a dove, holding in its beak a bunch of for-get-me-nots. A beautiful basket of flowers was in the center, with a dove nestling in their midst. An anchor, made of the choicest cuttings, was the gift of one of her dearest friends. A beautiful floral star rests on either side of the little mound, and a heart, cross and wreath lie by them. The funeral was largely attended, and a brief farewell was taken and a prayer offered at the cemetry. Undertaker Wiehl deserves great credit for the perfect manner in which everything was arranged.

Belle paid $825.00 for the property, with $400.00 down in cash. No longer would she pay rent and worry about a landlord who lived in fear he would be in trouble with the law for renting to her and could console himself only by raising the rent each month.

She again went to town, purchased more furniture and finery for the larger house, and immediately set to work to have it open as soon as possible. Mrs. Egbert recalled going by the house the evening of the grand opening. The yard was full of fancy-dressed women and men in tuxedos.

As her income grew, Belle began to speculate in stocks, bonds, and real estate. She was twenty-three years old, and she knew she had better make it while she could. For the rest of Daisy May's life, there would be the monthly payment for her board. She probably had the best advisors available from among her customers; and it was not long before she was very well off by most standards of the day, and especially considering where she had started only a few years earlier. She mortgaged, bought, sold, and reinvested with the best of them.

Money gave Belle another opportunity and pleasure. Remembering the months after her mother's death and the night she went, hungry, to Jennie Hill's, Belle was touched by the plight of those less fortunate than herself; no one in need was ever turned from her door without food or money.

In June of 1886, she purchased a twelve-grave lot in Calvary Cemetery and had her mother's body moved from the single grave lot in "potter's field." Over the grave, Belle had a large monument erected, as one would a family stone. On the side of the stone is inscribed:

Sarah McMeekin
Born May 5, 1836
Died May 19, 1876

Belle found that she was no longer satisfied with the dresses offered on the Lexington market and began shopping in Louisville, Cincinnati, and finally in New York, where she would check into one of the best hotels as Mrs. James Kenney. Food in the hotel dining room and in the fashionable restaurants was enjoyed and gave her ideas for the dinners she served the wealthy gentlemen who entertained their associates at "Belle's Place."

In the most expensive stores, she found the Paris fashions she brought back to dazzle the men and upset the women. Belle now dressed in a style as fine as the ladies in *Godey's Magazine* and *Peterson's Magazine*, whose pictures she had clipped from the periodicals and pasted in her scrapbook.

A bill for one of Belle's purchases was found years later back of her house in the trash pile. It was from the New York Store in Louisville, dated February 6, 1890, and showed she had purchased three pairs of ladies' drawers at $5.25 each — a goodly sum when a man's suit could be bought for slightly more and many women who appeared rather fashionable on the street were still wearing drawers made from feed sacks. After all, who would see them.

Another bill shows that Belle paid Madam C. Grunder, Modiste & Importer, 328 Fourth Avenue, Louisville, Kentucky, $18.00 for tailoring a garment, in addition to the cost of the finest materials and findings.

Furnishings in the house were constantly upgraded by purchases in Lexington, Cincinnati, and even New York. It was a time of change in styles; the ornate French Victorian and rococo revival were in vogue in Lexington, and Belle found them to have great appeal.

The girls, while they knew little about styles of furniture, did not fail to notice the effect the furnishings had on customers making their first visit. At one glance, a discerning gentleman knew he was in a "perty fancy whorehouse."

Men came and went, old girls moved on to what they hoped would be greener pastures as madams of their own houses, and new girls took their places. Some women took to drink, others to dope, and had to be sent away; but for the most part, they were sisters looked after by a kindly, but demanding, Belle. When it was necessary to dismiss a girl, it always hurt the young madam; and she usually gave her a good sum of money to help her get started in another town.

But the more prominent she became, the more the community wanted her scalp. She was charged with operating a "tipling house" or a "nuisance" twice in 1883, twice in 1884, and so on through the years. The fines ranged from $60.00 to $300.00; but Belle paid them without a whimper. They were part of the "cost of operation."

Studio photograph of Belle, showing the hourglass figure so fashionable at the time. Probably made just after she became a madam.

Studio photograph of Belle. She appears to be in her late twenties or early thirties.

For eight years she was located on North Upper across from Kentucky University (now Transylvania), but finally the pressure began to mount.

Charles C. Moore, a Christian minister whose church was in Versailles, Kentucky, had a most interesting experience that changed his life. He had a friend, son of the president of the University of Missouri, who was a professed infidel. Moore and the young man agreed not to argue their differences; Moore would read everything available on atheism, and his friend would read selections suggested by Moore on Christianity. Soon the friend was converted, and Moore baptized him on a Sunday in the Versailles church. But a few weeks later, after finishing his sermon, Moore put down his Bible, left the church, and informed his friends and family that he was an infidel. Each man had converted the other and lost his own beliefs in the process.

Moore came to Lexington (he had earlier inherited a large farm about eight miles from town) and, in order to prove that an infidel could be as moral as the next person, started "out-Christianing the Christians." He got a job on the paper and came down hard on liquor, tobacco, and horseracing (which almost got him killed on several occasions).

When the *Lexington Daily Press* came out on January 13, 1889, a front page article carried a "Petition of Citizens" demanding the closing of the "houses of ill fame conducted by Belle Breezing at 194 North Upper Street; Lettie Powell, 196 North Upper Street; and Molly Parker, 154 North Upper Street."

The petition was signed by thirty-three of Lexington's outstanding citizens. And lo, Charles C. Moore's name led all the rest.

Later, when the paper would no longer print his opinions, he started his own paper, *The Blue Grass Blade*, and was jailed several times for his views. In 1893, he was jailed for two months in Paris, Kentucky, for publishing a statement: "If I had a contract to bore for hell fire, I would build my derrick where the earth's crust is thinnest, in front of the Christian Church." Since he was jailed in Paris, this was evidently the location of the church he made reference to in his statement. He was later sentenced in Cincinnati to two years in the federal penitentiary in Ohio for blasphemy and while there wrote his second book, a most interesting story of his life entitled *Behind the Bars #31498* (Blue Grass Printing Co., Lexington, Ky., 1899).

Moore's later troubles didn't help Belle at the time, and it appeared her house would be closed. However, the authorities, taking a more realistic view, knew there would always be prostitution, if not in houses, then in the street where it would be harder to control.

CHAPTER 4

One For Money – One For Love

A few bawdy houses had opened in a colored section of town, and the city officials thought it a most likely spot to have a red light district. The location was Megowan Street. The area seemed ideal. Because there was no through traffic, persons traveling across town would not have to pass the houses; and the residents of the area were black and so had no voice for complaint. Belle had "hedged her bet" in 1888 by buying a small house on Dewees Street near that district. She rented it until such time as she might need it.

The old Megowan farm of "Belfast," when offered for sale as part of the estate in 1849, consisted of "a fine brick home, twenty-five acres of highly improved land with between 300 & 400 peach trees, one of the largest gardens in town furnishing vegetables to the Lexington Market all year round."

Belfast was sold, not for a home, but to speculators who sub-divided it; and streets were put in. Originally, it was expected to be a development of fine homes. Michael Foley, the grocer, purchased one of the first lots and built a two-story brick house, by far the best on Megowan Street, which was named after the elder Megowan. Others bought lots on the street and built large frame homes. Even-tually, the developers, finding sales slow for their lots, took advantage of the small land rush that occurred when colored soldiers who had served in the Union Army were finally granted pensions and had money to buy lots and build small frame houses.

As prostitutes and blacks began to move into the area, the genteel people sold their homes and moved to other locations. Foley, who probably had expended more on his house than the other owners, had difficulty in recouping his investment.

Miss Sue Green, who was one of the first madams to come to Megowan Street as the houses became available from their original owners, was charged in 1888 with "running a disorderly house" and fined $300.00. Several letters went off to Governor S. B. Buckner from irate men who considered this a travesty of justice.

Mat Walton wrote on stationery of the Ohio Centennial (where he was in charge of the Department of States):

> . . . I write you now at the urgent request of Miss Sue Green, an unfortunate lady of this City, who has been leading a sporting life– . . . Of course it is impossible to suppress houses of prostitution in a city the size of Lexington, and the policy of the State and City officials for several years has been to force them from the principal streets of the city, and from all decent neighborhoods, to such streets and parts of the city as are not inhabited by respectable people. In this they have succeeded. Miss. Green several years ago moved to Megowen street, which is peopled largely by the class above indicated– In fact it seems, by common consent given over to them– She has two children, a boy 11 years old, that is off at school and a daughter at the convent, being educated, and I am reliably informed that she is raising them as they should be– It necessarily takes a good deal of money to maintain and educate them, and she has a hard strugle to do this and to support herself. I am satisfied that the State is better able to loose it than she is to pay it– I think that you would act wisely to grant her a pardon. Believing that you will aid this lady, whose class receive but little sympathy from the world, I remain
>
> Yours very truly.
> Mat Walton

C. J. Bronston, using a Phoenix Hotel letterhead (he was a lawyer and also commonwealth attorney and must have chosen not to use his own stationery), wrote, in part:

> . . . Sue Green was indicted several years ago as keeping a bawdy house on Upper St. near Ky. University [now Transylvania] and at great sacrifice removed to the most obscure street in the city only occupied by negroes in small frame houses & the present indictment against her was on complaint of some of these negroes.

J. R. Morton, attorney, endorsed the letter as being his sentiments also.

J. C. Rogers, sheriff of Fayette County, wrote; but rather than mail the letter, he had it hand-delivered by Miss Sue Green herself. His letter reflects the same feelings as the others.

E. L. Hutchinson, Sue's lawyer, also sent her to Frankfort with a letter, which read, in part:

> . . . Her house is mortgaged. . . . Son in school. . . . daughter in convent. . . . Has a hard time keeping up her dues & interest in the building Association. . . . Her children will suffer.

S. G. Sharp, judge of Fayette County, also sent Sue to the governor.

> . . . This letter will be handed you by Miss Sue Green who is the proprietoress of a house of ill fame . . . on Megowan St. . . . The

best place for these poor misguided and miserable women. ... I officially know these women were advised to locate upon this particular street. ... There is only one piece of valuable residential property on the street & that is owned by a colored person.

Whether it was the pleas, the governor's soft heart, or the frequent trips Sue Green made to the governor's office is not known; but he granted a pardon.

This did not help poor Mike Foley, whose big brick house at the corner of Megowan and Wilson was not mentioned by Sue Green's champions. It is interesting to note that the Negroes were not considered in the decision to integrate their neighborhood with prostitutes.

The original of this picture of Belle hung in a gold leaf frame beside her bed in the house on Megowan Street.

It was at about this time that William M. Singerly entered the picture. A Philadelphia man who was interested in horses, he came to Lexington for the trotting horse meet each year. He was the proprietor of the *Philadelphia Record* (newspaper) and owned the street railway system in that city. He also owned a large brick yard, lumber yard and planing mill, knitting mill, paper mill, gleaning and binder factory, theaters, commercial buildings, over a thousand houses he had built and rented, and was president of two banks. He was a strong Democrat and had made an unsuccessful try for the governorship of the state. He also owned "Record Farm" in Montgomery County, Pennsylvania, a spread of seven hundred acres where he had what was then termed "the finest herd of Holstein cattle in America, as well as an extensive herd of high-grade Cotswold sheep." His biographical sketch, done in 1894, said, "He is a lover of horses, also, and in Kentucky is interested in a fine breed of trotting stock whose powers are being steadily improved."

Singerly had met Belle and found her delightful. Certainly a man of his standing had to watch his step at home, but not in Kentucky, and particularly at Belle's house, where his "powers were being steadily improved." When he heard of Charles C. Moore and the citizens' demands, he gave her a large sum of money (reported to be $50,000.00) to buy where she wouldn't be bothered and where he might find all the comforts of home when he came to Kentucky (and probably a few comforts he didn't have at home).

It has long been argued that Belle, with Singerly's money, built the house on the hill. But, in truth, she bought Foley's house at 59 Megowan Street and enlarged it. A study of the floor plan shows the house to have been a typical two-story residence of that time; and this was especially noticeable in the angles on the south side of the original front section. The original house probably had only eight rooms. After Belle's remodeling, it contained twenty or more rooms. (It is not certain what part of the attic was finished into living space.) It was not until 1895 that the third floor was added; the house then had twenty-seven rooms (including a kitchen and a room for parties in the basement).

The deed shows she paid Foley $1,400.00, certainly considerably more than a vacant 40 × 100 foot lot would be worth in a black section that was fast deteriorating and becoming the "designated" red light district.

So Charles Moore, the infidel, and his Christian cohorts won a round, Foley got rid of a house he no longer wanted, Belle got a larger house, and Singerly got what we hope was $50,000.00 worth of something.

Belle had the *Kentucky Leader* run the following ad on Sunday June 16, 1889:

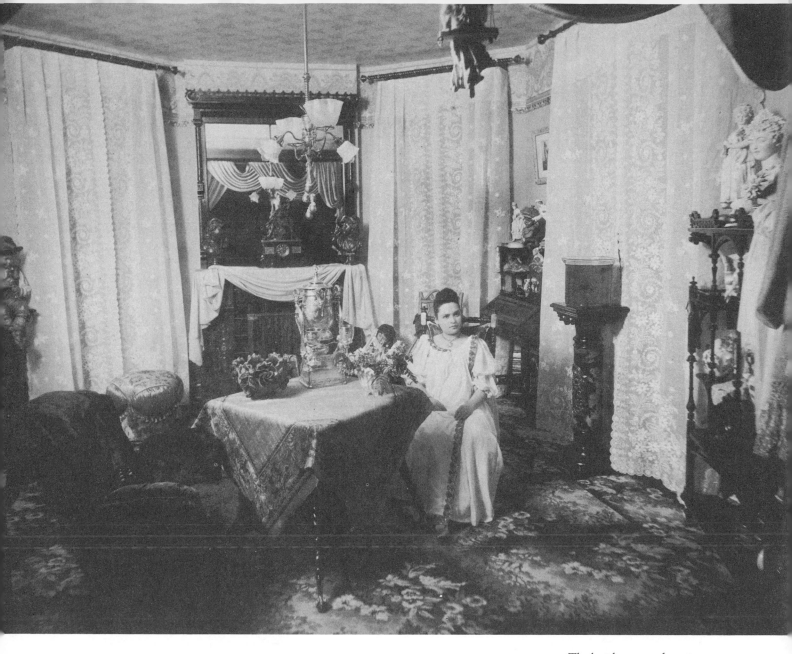

Take Notice.

As I am about to move from my present residence, I wish to have all my accounts settled at once. Those having bills against me please call and settle, and those owing me do the same. I am anxious to have all settled at once.

BELLE BREEZING.

This time there was no shortage of money, no mortgages, no restraint on what she bought. She had the cash to lay out, and she would do what Singerly wanted: open the "best damned whorehouse anybody ever saw."

Belle had never dreamed so fancy a house — more than she had ever hoped for — would be hers. She had once thought Jennie Hill's house the finest in the world. But wait till Lexington saw what she was going to create!

It would be more than a whorehouse; it would be a mansion for men, a gilded palace where a wealthy man could find whatever he wanted to fulfill his wildest fantasies. The food, the drink, and the girls would be the best to be had. The cares and worries that came with family and business would be shed at the door like a hair shirt, and pleasure would fill the night.

The table linens would be the finest, the china the most expensive, the food equal to what Belle had found in New York; and the service would be perfection. Furniture and decoration would be the latest, offering comfort to compare with the best men's clubs in the country. The body of the wine would be like a young girl's — firm, but yielding to a man of taste — and served in the finest crystal and cut glass, whose facets would fracture the light into all the colors of the rainbow. The girls would be dressed in evening gowns, and their undergarments would be of the finest silk fabric with lots of imported lace.

It is doubtful that Belle occupied either the house on Fourth Street or the one on Dewees, which she had purchased. Instead, she devoted the time after selling the property on North Upper to preparing for the opening of the big house on Megowan Street.

There has never been an opening night to eclipse Belle's. She had not yet gotten girls to her liking to fill all the rooms, so she invited several madams she had met from Louisville and Cincinnati to bring their girls and spend the weekend. Evening dress was required for both women and men, and the whole affair was "by invitation only." It was always said that engraved invitations were sent out, but this is doubtful. A mailed invitation might fall into the wrong hands. The invitations were probably more discreetly made. (It might be remembered that Belle Watling sent invitations. John Marsh must have recalled the stories he had heard in Lexington.)

Nothing was spared in design and decoration of the house. The floors were parquet of Honduran mahogany, native walnut, and light maple; Belle, giving her attention to every detail, selected the pattern to be used. Stained glass windows offered soft light, but no view from the street. The turned wood on the staircase, like the doors and facings throughout the house, was of rich walnut or cherry.

Chandeliers sported the newly-available electricity on alternate arms with gas jets, and all were ablaze. Mirrors reflected the lights and were, in turn, reflected again and again from other mirrors across the room, in the halls, or on the ceiling of the big dance room.

When all the decorating had been completed, Belle had a photographer come to the house and take pictures of a number of the rooms. These pictures have never before been published.

Downstairs parlor at Belle's with horn chair furniture given her by Texas admirer. The seats are upholstered in leopard skin. The painting on the summer fire screen is believed to be of Daisy May Kenney, Belle's daughter. The mantel scarves and tasselled draperies were considered the finest appointments for Victorian parlors.

View of Belle's private sitting room on the second floor. The child's rocker probably had been Daisy May's.

Belle's bedroom with the fine bedroom suite she bought at the 1894 Exposition.

A girl's room, possibly Pearl Hughes', one of Belle's favorite girls who later became her housekeeper.

Belle'e private sitting room on the second floor. The etagere contains some of Belle's extensive collection of bric-a-brac — items which sold for a nickel, a dime, or a quarter at the 1940 sale. The large vase in the doorway is an Imari import. The parlor lamp is on an onyx stand.

One of the downstairs parlors that opened into the dance room. The cuspidor and brass coal scuttle could be used by the girls to dispose of their drinks.

All the extra help that the kitchen could hold prepared food fit for kings. Beer was left in the cellar; it was a night for champagne. The only money that changed hands was in the form of tips to the girls. Food, wine, women, and song were "on the house."

Buggies passed all evening with the curious, the timid, and the uninvited who wanted a glimpse of the wildest party the town had ever seen. No one slept for blocks around, so loud was the music from the orchestra Belle had hired; and the shouts of men and the squealing and laughter of women went on until well after daylight.

Whether some of the Louisville and Cincinnati girls decided to stay in the fabulous house is not known, but from that day on there never seemed to be a shortage of girls at Belle's.

John Coyne, who had been a bartender in Lexington in the old days, told Meadors, "When you walked into Miss Belle's early in the evening, you would think you were in an embassy. The girls in evening dresses spoke no bad language and smoked no cigarettes on the first floor." Meadors said the old man's eyes misted with the memory.

The lamps were lighted, their chimneys and shades sparkling, and each reflected several times in the mirrors. In one glance, Belle could spot anything out of place or missing in the arrangement perfected long ago to contribute to the comfort of her guests and the enjoyment of the evening. Every night, it was like a fancy party. The girls in their evening dresses and Belle in one of her Paris fashions, resplendent with diamonds. The maid in a starched white apron, ready to open the door and take coats and hats.

Billy Mabon is first found in Belle's life in 1883. He must have been a regular customer of the house on Upper Street as a charge was made to his account in Belle's journal for two bottles of wine and pay for one of the girls. On March 4, 1888, Billy gave Belle a book inscribed to "Kitten," Billy's pet name for her. On Belle's thirty-second birthday, June 16, 1892, Billy gave her a lovely sterling silver spoon, with filigreed handle, engraved to "Kitten." He undoubtedly presented her with many other gifts over the years.

In the margin of the deed book in the Fayette County Court-house, there is a notation that an original deed, after being posted, was picked up for Belle by Billy Mabon in 1894. By this time, it is certain that he was no longer a customer who paid for whatever the house offered that he wanted.

Whether Billy became the usual "dandy man" is not of record, but he was Belle's boyfriend and served as her "outside representative." Where unscrupulous persons would take advantage of a woman, especially a madam, the dandy man was the one who could handle business matters and not fall prey to such people. In Belle's case, no one could best her; but it was easier to have Billy carry out her wishes.

Billy Mabon in Belle's private parlor.

It was the dandy man's job, or privilege, to break in new girls. A woman could become a wife with no previous experience, but a whore had to know what she was doing. Girls married as virgins with their only instructions coming from nervous mothers who, with their backs turned, said, "Do what he wants and get it over as quickly as possible." But the girls on the hill were there to give pleasure; that's what they were paid for, and that was what was expected.

A dandy man would take a new girl to her room and "show her how to treat a man properly." It stands to reason that some of the better-looking girls required more lessons than others. This service did not seem to affect the love relationship between the man and the madam. Whether Billy had the full role of "dandy" is not known.

In any case, Billy Mabon, who was regularly employed as a bookkeeper and auditor for the local water company, also kept Belle's financial affairs in order. He is seen in an early picture, sitting in her private parlor at her little Victorian drop front desk.

When Belle's "angel," Singerly, came to town, he would stop at the Phoenix Hotel and send a large bouquet of flowers to the house. When the flowers arrived, Belle would send Billy off to his apartment at 83 North Mill Street. This arrangement must have suited Billy, for he and Belle remained lovers over the years.

Belle once told her cook that it made her sick to see how some of the girls spent their money on men. "I never gave a man a nickel," she said. "With me it was the other way around. They gave me money." In any case, Billy always held a regular job and was self-supporting.

The girls of the house, usually deprived of true love, took great pleasure in Billy's demonstrations of affection for Miss Belle. When she returned home from a trip, Billy would have her rooms filled with flowers and stand by the curb, awaiting her carriage, to give her a big kiss — a sidewalk demonstration of his affection.

Billy upset his employers by being seen frequently riding about town with Belle. They called him on the carpet and informed him that the company he kept did not look good for the business. If it continued, they warned him, they would have to terminate his employment. Billy replied that they might as well fire him right then; he could get another job, but never another Belle. Jordan says there was a report that Miss Belle got together with "some of the Combses" and bought the water company so that Billy would not lose his job, but this cannot be confirmed.

Undoubtedly, Billy was a remarkable man. He could live with the knowledge of Belle's past and present and stand the treatment he was given, knowing she was the only woman in the world he could love. Perhaps they would have married, but Belle held fast to her Catholic belief and never divorced James Kenney.

James Tandy Ellis, the noted humorist, wrote to his friend at *The Lexington Herald* and said, in part:

> I always thought that a steamboat captain was the most envied man in the world until I saw the "Papa" at Belles. . . . and the way he swaggered in made him the Lord of creation. . . . Oh! to be a kept man with every whim gratified, and to be the Boss of Love, Laughter, wine & Song.

Ellis must have thought Billy ran the place, which was never the case; but it must be admitted that being a man among all those women would be considered by many an enviable position.

Belle's reference to the girls giving men their money was well-founded. Each girl was given a night off a week, and they usually went hopping with their "sweet men" to other houses on the hill. Sometimes they would go to Shouse's Bar and Beer Garden at the corner of Main and Dewees Streets. They would dance with the town boys or their "sweet men," but the girls were always the ones who paid the check. They were making more money than they ever dreamed of, and it flowed from them as easily as it came to them. Blanche Patterson, it is said, spent a fortune on a series of "sweet men."

Daisy May was now eighteen, and her mental condition was obviously not going to improve. Once more through the church, Belle arranged for Daisy's transfer to the House of the Good Shepherd on Fort Street in downtown Detroit, Michigan. The home had 345 inmates. Its stated purpose was "to restore fallen women to the path of virtue and to protect young girls who are liable to temptation from unfavorable surroundings." In addition to girls who fell under the above classification, who were sent to the home by the police or their guardians, a few feeble-minded girls were kept. Records show that most of the girls were literate, but Daisy could not read or write and was one of only a few who had no job assignment.

In order to protect the girls from identification and possible embarrassment, they were all given assumed names. Daisy, who had arrived under the name of Daisy Barnett, was given the name of Imelda Kinney. The responsible person was listed as Mrs. J. B. Kenney, Box 39, Lexington, Kentucky.

On February 15, 1908, when she was twenty-eight, Daisy was moved to a group of older women in the same institution, suggesting that she was no longer suited to the younger group.

There were several levels in the House of the Good Shepherd; and girls could, by their deeds, aspire to be elevated. Poor Daisy did not have the mental capacity to raise herself; but she could not have risen to the top and become a "sister," in any case, as the restrictions were very exacting. "No fallen woman can become a member of the order. This prohibition extends to a sister, niece, cousin or third generation descendant of a fallen woman."

Eventually, it seems Daisy was no longer suited to the House of the Good Shepherd because of her mental level. Accompanied by Sister Marie Theresa, she was transferred to St. Joseph's Retreat, also in Detroit, where she was accepted officially as a patient on May 27, 1913, under her real name of Daisy May Kenney.

CHAPTER 5

Phoenix

Things rolled along very well at 59 Megowan Street until Saturday, March 16, 1895. *The Press-Transcript* on March 17th reported the events of the preceding day.

MASS OF RUINS

IS MADAME BREEZING'S HOUSE ON MEGOWAN STREET.

Fire Breaks Out at 12 O'Clock and After an Hour and a Half the Building is in Ruins.

Madam Belle Breezing's magnificent house on Megowan street is now a mass of scorched and water-soaked ruins.

Yesterday morning, a few moments before the noon hour, fire broke out in the apartments of the proprietress from some unknown cause, and in a very few moments was communicated by the draperies to all of the upper part of the house. The flames rolled up the steps to the third story, and getting between the third story ceiling and the roof, were spread out under the whole roof.

The draperies and carpet caught and the flames ran down into the lower apartments, but did not do much damage there.

There were about fifteen or twenty women asleep in the house at the time, and as soon as the alarm was spread they rushed out, not having time to put on their clothes. The wildest excitement reigned among the inmates and the gathered crowd of spectators on the outside, when Flora Johnston, an inmate of the house, appeared at a window of a third-story room and screamed for help. The whole upper apartments were on fire and it was a matter of life and death with her in a very few moments. Some one in the crowd ran into the house and seized a mattress, and placing it on the ground under the window, told her to jump.

The frightened woman swung out the window, poised her body for a second or two on the sill, and then dropped to the mattress. She alighted on her back and was seriously shocked by the fall. She was taken to a house on the opposite side of the street, where Dr. Bosworth attended her injuries. She was seriously injured in the spine and it is probable that she will die.

Great volumes of smoke was rolling out every window in the house by the time the firemen arrived, but, after about an hour's struggle with the flames, succeeded in extinguishing them.

The upper stories are complete ruins while the furniture and lower walls and carpets were ruined by the water.

The house was considered the finest in the South and the loss has not as yet been estimated.

The proprietress was in New York at the time of the accident, but she was telegraphed for and will probably hurry home immediately.

The furniture was very rare and costly, and one set alone was worth about $1,500. There is about $40,000 insurance on the house and its furniture.

Tim Maher's Heroism.

Some one yelled during the progress of the fire that a costly set of diamonds were in a drawer in the third story, and Tim Maher, one of the firemen, siezed a ladder and putting it against the sill of an upper window entered the room amid the blinding smoke and rescued the diamonds. These were worth several hundred dollars.

Actually, the third floor described was only an attic, although Belle must have pressed it into service if someone was sleeping there.

This happened back in the good old days when the firewagons were horsedrawn and smoke and fire roared from the boilers as they charged down the street. A strong young lad could almost keep up with them. Everybody chased the firewagon, arriving on the scene as soon as possible. With the girls running around with few clothes on, the girl jumping to a mattress from far above (several fellows bragged for years that they were among the men who held the mattress), and the heroic young Tim Maher entering the smoke-filled room to save the diamonds (undoubtedly he was generously rewarded), this was an exciting event for the town, one that was talked about for years after.

When Belle came home, she shed not a tear. If she had tears, they would be kept inside with the ones from her childhood.

Work was begun immediately to restore the house, and Belle decided to add a full third floor. Business was good, and she could use the additional rooms. Whether there were bonuses for the workers or some extra incentives is not known, but no one had ever before seen a house completed with such speed. Since the new brick did not match the old, the entire house was painted white.

59 Megowan Street as it appeared about 1890 after Belle had added to the original house and before the fire of 1895.

After the fire of 1895 when the third floor was added at 59 Megowan Street. Belle had the house painted white to hide the obvious change in color of the new brick.

59 Megowan Street. Picture made after 1900. The white paint had begun to peel off. The differences in the brick are obvious, and the original roofline is discernible on the left. The house at this time was covered by trumpet vines.

It was not long before Belle's palace was reopened, grander than ever; and once again the music of black Tom West's fiddle and blind Negro John Boyce's guitar filled the night air on the hill.

Hacks came and went; and well-known gentlemen were frequently driven to the side door, known as the family entrance, where they could enter without being seen from the street or by other guests in the parlors (Belle remembered Jennie Hill's).

Local men often brought to Belle's the doves and other game they had killed on a hunt. She would have them prepared in the kitchen; and the hunter and his friends would return that evening to a gourmet meal served with fine wine and, if they desired, the girls of their choice.

Belle once told Squire J. Winston Coleman, Jr., a well-known Kentucky historian, that one of the secrets of her success was that she could manage three parties at one time and no one would know who was in the other groups. Stag parties, bachelor parties, birthdays, and promotions were all celebrated at Belle's. If a man made a killing at the track, he took his friends to party at the big house on the hill; and Belle got the winnings without the wager.

She installed every conceivable comfort and entertainment for her guests. Her music box stood nearly six feet high, and the large disks moved behind the beveled glass panels as if by magic as a new selection was called for. When player pianos came out, Belle had Johnny Mondelli (a local man who supplied coin-operated machines in the area) install the finest, with all the latest rolls.

Young boys would go up to Belle's in the late afternoon and dance with the girls. If they ran short of money, an old fellow told me, they put Tooloo gum on a nickel; and the piano would keep playing. Belle knew the young girls loved to dance and had been deprived of the good times that were gifted on the more fortunate. She would leave them alone until about 9:00 p.m. when she would come down and say, "Boys, you must go now. It's time for business."

A number of the girls opened their own houses as they grew older and found less demand for their personal services. Men would select the younger new girls, and the older women knew it was time to move on. Blanche Patterson, Pinkie Thomas, and many others learned their trade at Belle's and moved on to open other houses on the hill.

They all aspired to have a place as good as or better than Belle's, even if they were starting on a much smaller scale. Several took in girls who did not want to live up to the rules Miss Belle laid down. Some hated the dress code at the old house. They saw no reason to be dressed in an evening gown when they would probably be taking it off within the hour, only to have to redress completely before returning to the parlor, then back upstairs and undress again. This dressing and undressing might be repeated many times in one evening; and the girls thought kimonos, which were easily put on and taken off, were much less bothersome. Other restrictions — such as the ban on smoking in the parlors and lewd talk — at Miss Belle's were not to be found in the houses of the new madams.

The new places for the most part were little, one-story, "shotgun" houses. At Belle's, some of the girls' rooms were on the third floor. When a customer complained one night, the girl said, "Honey, if you can't climb the stairs, what the hell are you going to do when you get up there?"

Another of Belle's girls, after rendering service to eight men within a few hours on an especially busy night when the trot meet was on, sank into a chair and said, "God, them stairs is killin' me."

Rather than elevating their houses to glittering palaces, the new madams were destined to always operate little whorehouses. They never understood why they didn't have more customers and more income and never stopped to reflect that Belle had, by example, shown them the answer.

The smaller houses that clustered around 59 Megowan didn't bother Belle. In most cases, she was glad they were there to take in the undesirable customers she didn't want. But she hoped they would have a quiet operation. She knew when there was trouble on the hill it affected everyone. Bad publicity brought on a demand for reform and often resulted in public clamor to close the hill.

When R. P. Moloney, Sr., was a patrolman on the hill beat, Belle called him to the door one day to complain about a nearby house. "Those girls sit on the porch with their dress halfway up to their knees and talk to men passing by," she told him. "It's a disgrace and I want it stopped."

One of the interesting houses on the hill was run by "Mother"

Board. She had two beautiful young daughters, who were the only whores she kept. A number of references to "Mother" and her girls appear in the Jordan/Meadors interviews; but aside from her listing in the city directories (her house was at 148 Megowan), there is little additional information to be found. Perhaps they made their money and went back from whence they came.

The social climate at the time was responsible for rendering many men impotent. Not because of food or drink, but because of the tremendous burden of guilt placed upon them by the almost Puritan attitudes that prevailed. Perhaps the higher class of Belle's clientele can be attributed to the fact that there were a great number of socially prominent and wealthy men who felt that society demanded they treat their wives with almost the same respect with which they treated their mothers. This was probably as it should be, except in the case of sexual matters.

The only sexual instruction which most children received came in books, never from embarrassed parents; and the books, for the most part, were written by ministers who had little knowledge of life as it really existed. The following excerpts are typical of these books.

> After the honeymoon, which in all circumstances should last no longer than one month, no thoughtful husband will expect his wife to give herself to him except on some rare occasion or when another child is desired to make the home complete.
>
> No young wife can continue to love her husband if he uses her for self-gratification.
>
> Any man who shall frequently spill his seed will father only weak and imbecile children who in most cases will not survive more than one year.
>
> No refined young woman would think of disrobing in the room with her husband unless there is total darkness.

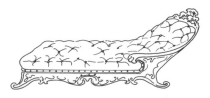

And so it was easy to understand the trembling hand of a first-nighter. Many men, married or single, had never seen a nude woman. To leave Belle's parlor and be led up the open staircase when everyone knew what one was going to do and, then, to watch

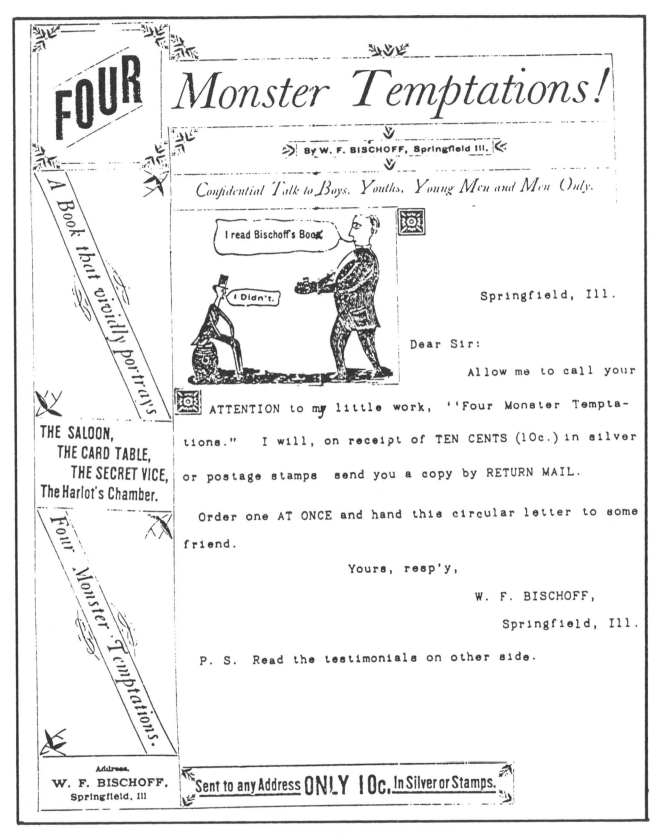

W. F. Bischoff, General Secretary of the Y.M.C.A., Springfield, Illinois, sent out the above circular in 1884.

a woman disrobe with the lights on and lie back on a couch or bed caused more than one man to forget how his clothes unbuttoned.

Later, hurrying down the street, trying to enter Main Street and the respectable community inconspicuously, the men checked and rechecked their apparel to be sure all was in order. They tried to block out of their minds their fear of perhaps having "caught something" and their guilt. If this could be done successfully, they felt they had then reached full manhood.

The quieting of fears of impotence, the relief from petting when a kiss was the expected climax of an evening with a "nice girl," the release of pent-up emotions for men married to frigid wives, the deliverance from the cares and torments that some men would carry to their graves — the girls gave a lot for a few dollars.

Belle and the girls were subjected to an insight into life that would have totally astounded most of the community.

Young men came who had never been with a woman before; frequently, they acted as if they were regulars at other houses. It was hard to keep the girls from laughing when, returning to the parlor, one of these fellows shook hands and thanked Belle and the girl who had just helped him lose his virginity. "Thank you, ma'am, it was nice to make your acquaintance. I hope we meet again."

Some touched Belle's heart. They were embarrassed, fearful, and oh, so naive. She would take the girl aside and tell her to be gentle. Even if their first experience was with a whore, it should be something pleasurable for them to remember in years to come.

When they had not been told before they arrived what the charge would be and found themselves with less than five dollars, Belle would frequently suggest another house where the price was lower, saying, "They have some very pretty girls over there."

They learned to lie about being on the hill, and it trained them for the business of life and the business of business.

As they got older, men came every year just to find out if they were still capable of performing the act. As time went on and they left after what they realized was their last visit, they looked as though they would cry. What had fulfilled them throughout their lives had been denied them — now it was over. More than anything else, it emphasized the inevitable aging process.

A prominent candy manufacturer died in bed with one of Belle's girls one night. As he arrived, he departed. Not wanting his wife and family embarrassed, his friends dressed him and deposited him on the porch at his home. It was hard on the same friends at the funeral when the preacher said, "What a wonderful way to die, coming home."

Although a number of girls from Belle's house married, others knew the proposals they received were made under the heady influence of sex and would be disastrous if acted on. One of Belle's girls told a young man who later reached considerable standing in the community, "I'd never make you a wife. Get up and ring the bell. Order us some champagne. Tonight we'll have a good time, and tomorrow you'll go on with your life and not be sorry."

A young man celebrating a raise or promotion at Belle's would brag to the girl about how much he made a week. The girls, who were instructed never to talk about their earnings, would not tell the ambitious young fellow that they made more than that a night.

In the same humorous letter mentioned earlier, Tandy Ellis wrote with regard to Belle's wealth:

> An old Scotchman had a son and a daughter. Both of them left home, and one day they returned. Jamie the son, was in rags, but Mamie, the daughter was dressed in silks and wore expensive jewelry. A neighbor said to the father, "I hear Mamie is a whore"? "I wish to God Jamie was a whore" said the father.

The Lexington Club was established in 1865 to provide a meeting place for selected gentlemen of the community. For many years, the club had rooms on the second floor of the Phoenix Hotel. Frequently, when a gentleman member needed transportation, he would telephone the club and have a waiter yell across the street to the hacks lined up there awaiting fares. It was an ideal spot for a hack stand — near the center of town, across from the hotel, and near the train station — and was improved with the opening of the Ben Ali Theater in 1913. On a Sunday afternoon, just as the crowd was leaving after a matinee, a waiter at the club called from the open window to a hack driver. "Bradford, Bradford! Mr. Stoll called and said come up to Miss Belle's and pick him up *right now!*"

Belle's clientele for the most part consisted of men of some means; it was not a place for customers who didn't have a bankroll to spend. An elderly gentleman, who had farmed in the Blue Grass all his life, told me he never went to Belle's. "I would go around on Wilson Street to one of those smaller houses where I felt more at home."

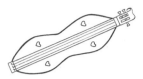

Belle always made a special effort to see that her girls had a nice Christmas. She could not forget the loneliness that surrounded her when she had gone to Jennie Hill's on that cold Christmas Eve in 1879. For many of the girls, this was their first Christmas away from their families; and Christmas time brought memories of childhood. Although they knew they were no longer welcome there, they felt a longing for home. It was to this sadness that Belle addressed herself. In addition to the tree, the food, and the gifts, she always attempted to have some special surprise.

John Jacob Niles, who years later became a concert artist, arranger of folk music, and composer and who was described by *Time* magazine as "the dean of American balladiers," was a young man of twenty in 1912 when he received a call from Miss Belle. Later, he would appear as a soloist at Carnegic Hall in New York and Grothrian Hall in London; but in his *Autobiography of John Jacob Niles: the Early Years* (Vol. I), an unpublished manuscript copyrighted in 1982 by the John Jacob Niles Estate and kindly made available by Mrs. Niles, the musician reveals that, when he was a young man working in Lexington, his music was sometimes heard in less lofty places.

> I encountered a bank clerk who told me of a chance I might have to play piano in a saloon on Limestone Street. . . . Someone had given the operator of this bar a smallish grand piano, and he had already engaged a player who claimed he could manage trumpet or trombone, a very versatile drummer who could double with the comb and the xylophone, an old-time fiddler who could play with the instrument under his chin or mountain style flat on his chest, and now he had a "piano player". . . . The saloon paid me a dollar a night and all the beer and food I could consume.
>
> Up to that time I had never played piano or sung my music in a brothel, but that seemed to be my next move, because I had a discreet telephone call from the most widely known madame in all our area, an invitation to call at her house at my earliest convenience to discuss a performance of music. So it was that on my very first free night, I walked up to the intersection of McGowen and Wilson Streets. . . . I announced myself to that handsome black man who seemed to be the official doorman (a one-time sparring partner of Bob Fitzsimmons) and presently I was received by the famous Madame. There was no beating around the bush with Belle Breezing. In fact, she came to the point. . . .
>
> "I have been given to understand that you are a singer and a musician," said she. "That you recently charmed Christ Church when one of the regular choir people was out of voice."

To all this I nodded, and she went on, . . . "[T]o make short work of all this, I am hoping to engage a quartet of singers". . . .

"A mixed quartet," said I. . . .

"Not the male quartet," said she quickly. "I want two girls and two men singing, . . . and I want the singing to start early. Seven o'clock. Can you sing that early?"

I explained that I had sung at 4 A.M. in Catholic churches. Seven A.M. would be quite easy.

"I am prepared to pay the singers five dollars apiece, and will provide a Christmas breakfast that they will remember." And then, after a pause, she asked, "Do you think they will sing for five dollars? You must know that five dollars goes a long way in a house like mine."

We laughed at that remark and I said, "Ma'am, I accept your offer."

Being not yet twenty-one, I thought it would be a lark to sing in one of America's greatest whorehouses. But I knew . . . I would have to work some kind of modern miracle to trap three others into joining me to sing the birth of Our Lord . . . in the confines of a house of ill fame of all things, on Christmas morning! . . .

I knew exactly what I was getting into, and I loved it. If I couldn't recruit a quartet, I decided to sing it alone. . . .

The performance was solo and a capella. The girls hung out the doors of their rooms and oohed and aahed at me as I walked past singing. Miss Belle was there beside me. . . . Then it was over, and Miss Belle, who said that her own breakfast was usually very light, sat at the head of that long table, and I sat on her right. From time to time, the girls, now dressed quite like great ladies, came timidly and ate ravenously, giggled like boarding school girls. . . .

When Miss Belle rose, everyone else rose. She accompanied me to the door and handed me an envelope, which I later discovered to contain exactly twenty-five dollars. She had planned to pay the quartet twenty dollars, but when I was called upon to sing alone, she raised the fee to twenty-five. I bundled up and walked slowly and decided not to tell anyone anything. . . . My twenty-five dollars bought me the winter overcoat I needed so badly.

Later in the morning, the girls exchanged gifts, and each received a lovely present from Miss Belle. It was always a festive occasion that helped to dispel the gloom they would have felt had Belle not planned ahead for her girls. When it came time to give out the gifts, there was always a fine representation of prominent men who had brought gifts for their regular girls and for Miss Belle. A well-known Lexington banker always dressed up (he didn't need padding) and played Santa Claus.

When they could no longer stand the rejection or, worse, the martyred submission when they asked for sexual favors from wives (whose pleasure was in not having pleasure), they came to Belle's; frequently, they later felt remorse that they could not control what they had always been told were animal instincts. Many a wife, unknowingly, had Belle to thank for the piece of jewelry she received from her guilt-ridden husband.

Sometimes, the guilt after being with a prostitute was overwhelming, especially for those whose Victorian convictions for the most part controlled their lives. Boston Corbett, the religious fanatic who shot John Wilkes Booth, came back to his quarters after visiting a prostitute in Washington, D.C., and, overcome with remorse, castrated himself.

Lexington newspapers, borrowing from big city tabloids, frequently referred to the local red light district as "the tenderloin section." The name referred to the handouts and bribes granted in such sections and indicated that cops on these beats were the only ones who could afford the better cuts of meat. "The hill" was a choice assignment, as Belle's kitchen was always open to an officer of the law for a good meal or a cup of hot coffee on cold nights.

The cop on the beat could be depended on to help restore order, dispatch drunks, or perform other chores; he was always in Belle's debt. She saw to that.

Sometimes, when it was known in advance that someone intended to go to the grand jury to try to have the hill closed, Belle would be tipped off. She would pass the word to the other houses, and they would all keep things quiet until the pressure was off. Belle's influence and judgment made her the unofficial mayor of the hill. When trouble in any of the houses brought a police investigation, she was no doubt upset. Such incidents reflected on all the houses.

One summer night, when it was exceptionally warm, Pearl and some of the girls went out to sit on the front porch and steps. This was probably very late at night since Belle did not allow anyone to sit on the front porch looking as if she were trying to attract customers.

Two men, who were quite drunk, came by waving a pistol and yelling that they were hunting for a cop to shoot. Shortly after they left, Patrolman Ed Tincher came by. Pearl told him of the incident and remarked she was glad he had not been there as he might have been shot.

While Tincher was talking to the girls, the men came back down the street. Pearl started to herd the girls into the house, but Tincher told them to stay where they were as he stepped over into the shadows. When the men got in front of the house, they started shooting the pistol off in the air. Tincher slipped around behind the man with the gun, gave him a big bear hug, and wrenched the pistol from his hand. It was the latest model Colt pistol; men considered it a very desirable gun for those who could afford one (Tincher, on his salary, couldn't).

As the second man ran off down the street, Tincher told the gunman, "You're my prisoner. You stand up against this wall while I go get the other fellow."

Pearl said Ed then went down the street and was gone quite a while. When he came back, he asked Pearl where his prisoner was. She replied, "I figure he must be in the next county by now."

In early 1898, William M. Singerly's empire began to crumble. Belle's "angel" saw his mills running at a financial loss, but he kept them open in the best interest of his employees. His other business interests began to falter, and his wealth could not keep him afloat. Soon after his two banks failed, his heart followed suit; he died in the early afternoon of February 27, 1898.

He had been a great asset to Philadelphia and was liked or loved by a great number of persons who had been the beneficiaries of his charitable works.

The family received messages of condolence from people all over the country, including governors and senators, as well as Presidents Arthur, Cleveland, Harrison, and McKinley. Everyone spoke of his generosity, but it is doubtful if any of them knew how he had helped a girl in Lexington, Kentucky, when her adversaries thought they had at last found the power to drive her from their town. Who knows but that he might have died much sooner had his heart not had the gentle exercise it received at his Kentucky spa.

Belle read the account of the death in the morning *Herald* the next day. She surely must have had a great feeling for this man who had been her benefactor. Although Singerly was thirty years her senior, they had each found something in the other that led to a common bond. Singerly, who had earlier had two wives, could have had almost any woman he wanted; and Belle's independence was strong enough to reject his money if she had found him otherwise undesirable. His generosity spoke well of him; and hundreds, if not thousands, of people who had nothing to offer in return were helped by his great wealth. When he was with Belle, it is reasonable to assume he had no reason to regret his kindness to her. Belle's generosity, though certainly on a smaller scale, was in proportion to Singerly's; they both demonstrated their feeling for those less fortunate.

The late Phil Minor (a true gentleman and well-known book-maker in Lexington), once told me that men from two local Irish families (he wouldn't give their names, saying they were still prominent in town) met at Belle's one night when Singerly was there. As they drank, they began to argue (as many Irish are wont to do); soon a fight broke out. Belle had someone call the policeman on the beat. The men were about to be thrown out when Singerly said, "Let them go at it. I'll pay for any damage they do." Belle sent the officer away as the men continued fighting. Phil said they broke up furniture, pictures, mirrors, and ornaments. They fought on all three floors and the staircases between. Finally, when all were worn out, they had another drink and left together, singing as they held each other up going down the hill to Main Street. The next morning Singerly gave Belle a check for $10,000.00 as he left, saying he had never had a more enjoyable evening.

The beginning of the Spanish American War in 1898 brought soldiers to Lexington and customers to Belle's. There were two large training camps near town. While the enlisted men flooded the other houses on the hill, Belle entertained the officers. Her "mansion for men" was well-equipped to serve exceptional meals, arrange parties, and cater to the other desires of the young men who thought the little war quite a lark and were delighted to find this "home away from home." The elite had been given officer status; they were, for the most part, from wealthy families and did not need to rely solely on Army pay.

The war lasted only eight months, but Belle banked a fortune. Soldiers returning home told of this fabulous bawdy house, and Belle began to enjoy a national reputation.

CHAPTER 6

Good Days — Bad Days

Belle remembered when there was an excitement that came with opening time — Who would show up tonight? Who would be good for a few laughs after he left? Would there be some new faces, perhaps a young boy just turning to manhood? Would there be a man from the track with plenty to spend?

For Belle, it was not as it once had been. She didn't need the money, but she was on a roll and couldn't stop. Still, she liked to see the excitement in her girls. It was good for business.

Over the years, it had taken a lot of hard work to keep her house running smoothly and successfully. Now, when the money didn't matter, she couldn't just sit with her memories and talk about "the way it used to be." That, to Belle, was unthinkable; it would be like dying by degrees — admitting you were finished.

Inside her, behind a dam of pride and stubbornness, there was a lifetime of pain and tears. Shedding them at the time would have given someone satisfaction, and she would not grant tears like that to anyone. Seldom had they been allowed to advance to where she felt their sting in her eyes; and not since she was a child had she let them flow, even in private.

She remembered a story in Papa Brezing's German book about the child who looked back and lost a step to the wolves that chased her. Belle felt like that girl: If she showed weakness, the wolves were waiting.

Now there was a weakness in her; even if at first she wouldn't admit it, she knew it was there. It had started some years before, partly for excitement and partly to give relief from the memories that continued to plague her, thoughts of things past that she could not change. First, it took just a little morphine to give the results she sought. She would go for days without it to convince herself she was not addicted; but if troubles pressed in, she knew it was there; and she began to use it more freely.

This was before the Harrison Narcotic Act of 1914, and morphine was easily purchased at the corner drugstore. When Belle realized she was "hooked," she made frequent attempts to break the habit. Dr. C. A. Nevitt said she would enter his sanitarium, and he would reduce her doses until she would be taking very little. Then she would hemorrhage, and he would have to give her more. Her normal dose was twelve and a half grains a day, and she would often be able to get along on this level for long periods. She still functioned well, and the operation of the house was not affected.

Her strength had been in her understanding of the weaknesses in others. There were four things that would satisfy men; usually, only one was needed. Flattery cost her nothing. Food always made men feel good, and its secret lay in its preparation and service; some could linger over meals for an entire evening. Sex her girls were well-equipped to furnish. But most important was that insatiable need for power, and that she had paid most particular attention to over the years.

She had contributed to more political campaigns than many a "king maker"; and since her handouts were never acknowledged nor spoken of, she could donate to both sides, thus insuring that the winner would be in no position to adversely affect her operation. If public sentiment demanded a crackdown, it was never so severe that her lawyer could not handle it without requiring her appearance in court. She was no fool; she learned to carve out a place for herself within the system. As these men left with a pocket stuffed full of her hard-earned money, she probably wondered, "Which of us is the whore?"

Belle outfitted her girls with clothes from a number of Lexington stores: Embry's, Meyers', Strauss', and the Mistresses Nugent and Shannon. She would contact the stores in the afternoon, asking if it would be convenient for her to bring the girls in after store hours. Permission was always given since the sales made in these few hours would usually exceed the receipts for the whole week.

The procession, with her carriage and whatever additional hacks were needed, would leave the hill just after the shops had closed when most of the townspeople were at home for the dinner hour. The carriages would turn down Main toward their destination. Arriving at the store, the girls were hurriedly ushered in. A chair would be brought for Belle while the girls went into the fitting rooms. As the girls came out with the dress or dresses of their choice, Belle would pass on them. If she approved, she would post the amount to the girls' accounts.

Mr. Meyers would keep some of the salesgirls after hours to help with the fittings and caution his employees "I don't want any staring. I don't want any snickering. You treat them just like you treat every other customer. Belle Brezing pays cash, and these racehorse farms won't pay for a year."

Although she kept them well-dressed and they were making money, Belle always seemed mindful that her girls were young and that they were missing much of life. Things she had missed as she struggled to make a life for herself from the ruins of her childhood.

Frequently, she would take some of the girls to the old Opera House to see a stage play or minstrel show. She avoided that time before the show when friends greeted friends and the aisles were full. She and the girls, all as beautifully dressed as anyone present, would enter just before the curtain went up, never failing to elicit an audible gasp from the audience. The stage could have their attention when the house lights went down; for that short minute, their attention belonged to Belle.

During the races, she would take the girls (before business hours started on the hill) to her private box to watch the horses run and to be watched by the crowd. Once in their chairs, they never moved until it was time to leave. Their bets were sent down by a servant Belle would bring or by her bodyguard. Belle was not in fear of her life, but there was always a chance someone would start trouble, and it was her guard's duty to see that she was whisked from the scene. William H. Townsend, a Kentucky historian, said her bodyguard, who also acted as bouncer at the house, had been a sparring partner for both Jim Corbett and Bob Fitzsimmons.

Morning was the quiet time. The girls slept late, and Belle never rose before eleven or twelve unless she had a business appointment. Billy would slip out of bed, shave, and dress without rousing her.

Then he went down to the kitchen where Pearl Hughes (it was said she took her name from Tandy Hughes) would have breakfast started. Pearl was always the last to go to bed after the house was locked for the night and the first to rise in the morning. It seemed she never slept. Although she was the housekeeper and cooking was not her job, she could never wait for the slow help to arrive. The fact that Billy and Pearl both loved Belle gave them something in common, and each was comfortable in the other's company.

It hardly seemed possible that this kitchen, so filled with the warmth of the early morning sun, was part of the same house that had been the scene of so much revelry the night before. The ashtrays, with their stinking butts, were always emptied at night; but the smell of what had been the best Havana cigars lingered. This was offensive to Pearl; and she always opened the windows before she went to the kitchen, flooding the house with the clean, early morning air.

If gentlemen had stayed the night, they usually found their way downstairs, led by the aroma of coffee and frying ham. These men — sleepy, hungover, and probably fighting an internal war with their consciences — were not fit company; and Billy would hurriedly leave for work when they made an appearance. Pearl made sure the men were fed, saw to it that they had plenty of coffee, and got them a hack if they wanted one.

Ernest Featherstone, who made and spent big money in the trotting horse business, once told Meadors of an occasion when he was preparing to leave Belle's house after an evening of enjoyment. It was around midnight, and both Belle and Pearl advised him that he was too drunk to go out. Afraid he might pass out in the street, or possibly be arrested, they persuaded him to remain at the house that night for his own sake. He protested, saying he had to be at the trotting track early the next morning to see a horse he was trying to sell work out.

"That's all right," said Pearl. "Just tell me what time you have to be at the track, and I'll guarantee to get you up in time and see that you get there."

She put him to bed in an unoccupied room; and at about five

o'clock the next morning, she woke him. Pearl first gave him a small drink of whiskey — "I needed it," he said — and then gave him two cups of strong coffee. She had already brushed his clothes and cleaned his shoes. She fed him a good breakfast, along with more coffee. Pearl had also arranged for a horsedrawn hack to be waiting. He got to the track, made his appointment, and later sold the horse.

Featherstone told Meadors, "Pearl was one of the best la. . . . ." He had started to say "ladies," but stopped short and started over, saying she was "one of the best whores" he ever knew. Pearl had been a "girl" in Belle's house before she grew too old for the trade and had stayed on as housekeeper.

As the sun climbed higher in the sky, the girls began to drift into the kitchen for breakfast. The milkman and the iceman would stop in to make their deliveries and ask Pearl for a cup of coffee. Sitting around the big table, they would talk with the girls. If the conversation became too rowdy, or if one of the girls came near mentioning the name of a customer, Pearl had only to clear her throat; and stories were left untold.

On Sunday mornings, after a busy Saturday night, the girls slept especially late. The Negro children in the neighborhood soon found that, if they played along Wilson Street beside the house, the girls would throw them coins from the upper windows on the promise they would leave. As old men, they told with a chuckle how they "got their pennies for candy."

The cleaning girls, under Pearl's watchful eye, started their work downstairs and went from room to room cleaning, dusting, and putting everything in the order Belle expected and Pearl demanded. All the finer pieces of bric-a-brac were left for Pearl, as she didn't trust Miss Belle's best things to "careless help." Pearl's position was housekeeper; but anyone who was around for long found out she was, more accurately, the house's resident manager, second in command; and no one crossed her.

Belle would sometimes ring the kitchen for her breakfast to be brought up. She had installed a bell system in each room, which was connected to the kitchen. Pointers indicated the room wanting service. At other times, she would appear in her dressing gown to be served in the smaller dining room. She never asked Pearl about the day-to-day care of the house, but would usually plan menus with her. Belle was left free of the daily routine and devoted her attention to the night and seeing to the comfort of the guests.

In later years, when Belle's drug addiction demanded more frequent shots, Pearl prepared everything and placed it on a tray beside her bed. But she could never bear to watch as Belle put the needle into her arm. Although it broke her heart, Pearl accepted Belle's need as insurmountable, but refused to witness the mechanics of it.

Many of the girls who came to ask if they might "board" at Belle's were screened by Pearl before ever speaking with the madam. If they met Pearl's standards, they were sent on to Belle. They would find her questions sharp and to the point. If one of them hesitated too long before answering a query, Belle often rejected her. Belle ran the most prestigious of all the "boarding houses," and there were plenty of girls who wanted to be at "Miss Belle's." There was no need to take on dimwits who could not carry on a simple conversation.

Belle always asked those who came if they were virgins. If the answer was "Yes," she would say, "I cannot use you. This is no place for virgins."

There were a number of roads that led to prostitution.

Some women found themselves without money or the skills to earn it. Some were left stranded by husbands who died or deserted them. Others were turned out of their homes for transgressions.

Belle said that as long as there were cruel fathers she would have little trouble getting girls. Young girls caught "in the haystack" were frequently barred from their homes by their fathers, and many of these girls ended up on the hill.

On a summer evening, a lovely young girl from near Paris, Kentucky, finally gave in to the pleas of her boyfriend. The young man, son of a wealthy landowner, lived on the adjoining farm. The two had gone to school together, and the girl believed his promises of marriage.

As they lay on the soft needles beneath a hemlock on the bank of Stoner Creek, the girl's father, a suspicious man who gave constant attention to his daughter's movements, caught them "in the act." The boy, in fear for his life, pled that the girl had enticed him, grabbed his clothes, and without stopping to put them on, fled across the fields. The father, after giving his daughter a severe beating, sent her off with only the clothes she picked up from under the tree, warning her never to come back.

There was no one for the girl to turn to. The boy, who was asserting his undying love an hour ago, had now deserted her. On that one night in the space of a few minutes, she had lost her virginity, her lover, her family, and her home.

In the moonlight, she cried as she walked the weary miles to Lexington. Arriving at Main Street, she was stopped and questioned by the night patrolman. She would not tell him her name or where she had come from; and the officer, sensing that she had suffered some tragedy, decided not to "run her in." She asked where she might "board," which meant one thing to her and quite another to the patrolman. He directed her to the hill, telling her they were all boarding houses; and just past dawn, she wearily climbed the steps at 59 Megowan Street. There were no "boarding" signs as she had expected, but she chose the house because it was the largest and most respectable looking on the street, more like a hotel in the eyes of this country girl. It wasn't until after she had hesitantly rapped on the door that a suspicion entered her mind as to where she was. Distraught, she almost turned to run down the steps; but the fact that there was nowhere else to go kept her there, hesitantly awaiting whatever life now held for her.

She had wondered as she walked those tiring miles how she could pay board, whether it was expected in advance, how she could get a job. All she knew was cooking and cleaning. Now another fear was heaped on her almost unbearable load.

At that moment Pearl, who was the only one up so early, answered the door. Looking at the girl's condition, she asked her in without questions. She was led to the kitchen, shown where to wash up, and promptly given food. The kindness exhibited by the older woman, together with her own footsore weariness, brought forth her story.

Pearl listened quietly until the girl had finished. It was a story she had undoubtedly heard, with slight variations, before. Tears were mingled with each word; and when the girl had told it all, she was still racked with sobs. Pearl, sitting across the table from her, pressed her hand, not saying a word. When the girl stopped, Pearl explained where she was and suggested that she rest before making a decision on what to do. Shown into an empty room, she fell exhausted on the bed and slept until afternoon.

When she finally awoke, she was taken to Belle. Before she entered Belle's sitting room, she had made up her mind. Her father had shouted that she was a whore the night before, and now she was going to become one. She was a beautiful girl, determined to stay; and Belle was glad to have her.

It was almost two years later when she first heard from home. A cousin, who had been told where she was, came one afternoon to tell her that her mother lay dying and was asking for her. Hurriedly, she left with the messenger. When the buggy pulled up in front of her house, her father was standing on the porch. He must have been told she had been sent for. "Don't get down," he said. "You're not coming in this house."

She was angry. She wished she could jump down and beat this horrible man whom she had once loved. She knew she could not, so she begged. "Please let me go to Mother," she cried. "I'll only be a minute and I'll never come back again."

"No, whore!" her father shouted. "Get off my property!"

The boy snapped the reins, and the girl went sobbing back to Belle's. That night her mother died.

Another year passed, and her brother came to Belle's to ask for her, telling her that her father was on his deathbed and had asked her to come so he could forgive her.

"Him forgive me?" she asked through clenched teeth. "The bastard wants me to forgive him! You tell him I'll see him in hell."

Sadness stayed with her, and like a shadow it seemed to darken her eyes. She was more beautiful at twenty-two than she had been at eighteen. She did not have the quick laughter of the other girls, but there was a thrill that excited the recipient of her soft smile.

Her story was often told on the hill; it had all the elements to satisfy other girls who had suffered at the hands of cruel fathers. Best of all, it had a perfect ending. She married a man from California, who provided her with her own home where she had a new life.

Maybe this was the end of the story; maybe she did "live happily ever after." But a study made in Chicago in 1911 by the Vice Commission, whose report, "The Social Evil in Chicago," was printed that year by Guthorp-Warren, reports that "white slave" traffic was prominent in the country. Girls were taken to California on various pretexts and were then forced on to ships and sent to China, where it was said many wealthy Chinese preferred Caucasian women. Pimps or procurers (they were called "cadets" in Chicago) were paid well for young and beautiful prostitutes obtained for this trade. The Chicago report says most were taken to Macao in southern China, where they were placed in houses.

Perhaps in an unmarked grave in this far-off place, along the Chu Kiang River, lie the remains of a Bourbon County girl.

Prostitutes often called themselves "dressmakers" when forced to explain themselves to any kind of officialdom. Belle's mother is listed as a dressmaker in city directories which appeared after she and McMeekin parted. After all, most girls could sew then; and it was hard for them to show any "visible means of support," a standard used by the police to determine if a woman was a prostitute.

Around 1897, just before election time, the Lexington police were instructed by the incumbents, who needed to show they were all good guys, to round up all the city's prostitutes. The girls were brought in and appeared before Judge John J. Riley, who was known to be sympathetic. (He married a girl from Belle's house after the death of his first wife.) Pressure was being applied on the judge to be more severe, and the newspapers were stirring up public sentiment to have him removed from the bench. (He was charged in 1894 with malfeasance in office, but he beat the rap.)

As each girl was brought before him, he asked her occupation; and each, in turn, replied "Dressmaker." Judge Riley then assessed each a small fine, with the knowledge that she could easily make up the loss later that night. Finally, one girl whom the judge knew quite well was brought before him.

"What's your occupation?" he asked.

"Judge," she replied, "you know I'm a whore."

When the boisterous laughter in the courtroom subsided, Judge Riley leaned closer and, with a twinkle in his eye, inquired, "How's business?"

This brought more peals of laughter from the gallery; and the girl, without batting an eye, said "Lousy as hell, Judge, with all these dressmakers around."

The roar that went up at this drowned out all else; so when Judge Riley said, "Dismissed," only those near the bench could hear him.

Judge Riley, who was a sort of protector of the girls on the hill (as the preceding "dressmakers" incident shows), was obviously in a sad mood when he showed up at the police station one day. Ella Childers, who weighed about three hundred pounds, had died. She was not one of Belle's girls, but was in a cheaper house in the district. The judge had undertaken to see that she had a decent funeral, and the next order of business was to get pallbearers.

Dennie McCarthy, a police captain, told the story to Joe Jordan years later. He said Judge Riley remarked at the station that poor Ella Childers had died and that she should have a decent funeral and burial. Dennie, Detective Dudley B. Veal, and Pete Jenkins, a policeman, all chimed in piously and agreed with His Honor that it would indeed be a shame if she were not put away in a civilized, Christian fashion.

"All right," said Riley. "If that's the way you feel about it, I want you to act as pallbearers." They squirmed; but he insisted, telling them they were hypocrites, just saying that the poor girl ought to have a decent funeral and then not being willing to do their parts. They didn't like it, but they had committed themselves. Besides, they were all three members of the police department and more or less had to stay in favor with the police judge.

The judge next put the bee on "Bosco" Worsham, who, unlike the others, was not a policeman. In fact, he was not long out of the penitentiary. "I can't do it, Judge," the ex-convict said. "I got my reputation to think about." But Riley put the pressure on, and Bosco finally gave up and agreed to serve. Then he got two others, whose names McCarthy had forgotten.

Ella was so big she had to have an oversize coffin. The undertaker got it through the front door into the whorehouse all right when it was empty, by turning it with one side up. But it couldn't be handled that way with her in it. However, they found a first-floor window that was wide enough and, with some extra help, passed it out the window and got it into the hearse.

Then they started down Main Street to the Lexington Cemetery. The pallbearers at first pulled the blinds down in their carriage; they were ashamed to be seen in the whore's funeral procession. But they soon got over that and started inching the blinds up; and by the time they got downtown, they had them all the way up and were speaking to acquaintances on the sidewalk.

A fellow standing in front of the poolroom yelled, "Hey, Bosco! Who's dead?"

"One of the girls up on the hill," Bosco yelled back. "I didn't know her myself, but they say she was a real nice girl."

When they got to the grave, the six pallbearers had no extra help; and they had quite a struggle. Judge Riley and the preacher were pacing along beside them. It had been raining; and as they walked across the grass from the driveway to the grave, Dennie said, their feet were sinking deep in the soft ground, so heavy was their burden.

"Pull up. You're not lifting your part," one pallbearer spoke across the coffin to another.

"Pull up yourself, you bastard," was the reply. "I'm lifting more than you are."

This greatly embarrassed Judge Riley because of the presence of the preacher, and he frowned and shushed the boys.

When they finally got the coffin resting on the straps across the open grave, they straightened up in relief. The coffin handle had made deep creases inside the fingers of Bosco's right hand. Just as the preacher, with his book open, looked around to get everyone's attention before he started reading, Bosco arched his aching back, rubbed the fingers of his right hand vigorously with his left hand, and said, loud and plain, "Jesus Christ! Wasn't she a heavy son of a bitch?"

With few exceptions, Belle's house was, as *Time* magazine put it, "the most orderly of disorderly houses." One of these exceptions occurred in 1911.

In a whorehouse, the danger always existed of a man falling in love with one of the girls. The customers sometimes forgot they were paying for the attention they received, and the fine line between passion and love was occasionally crossed with disastrous results. Balzac said, "A young man loves the first woman who flatters him"; and flattery was part of the service.

On an oppressively hot night in July of 1911, Oliver Broaddus, a young man who worked as a butcher in the old Market House and was, as they say, "mean when drunk," found Debbie Harvey, whom he considered "his" girl, talking to two men in the parlor at Belle's. Broaddus called Debbie away from the men and took her into a room off the hallway.

They had been there only a short time when Belle heard screams. She ran into the room and saw Broaddus kneeling over the prostrate body of the girl, twisting a knife in her throat. Debbie cried out, "He's killing me."

Belle seized Broaddus by his collar and attempted to pull him away from the girl, but he leaped to his feet; and Belle, believing he was going to attack her, ran from the room to summon help.

A deep stab just above the left collarbone, near the juncture of the breastbone, ranged downward and back and had severed young Debbie's aorta.

In addition to the fatal stab, it was found that several other slashes had been cut in her breast and arms, while three of her fingers were cut to the bone, indicating she had made a desperate attempt to gain possession of the knife.

As Belle screamed, the entire house erupted in turmoil. Women ran to hide; men fled in all directions; and in the confusion, Broaddus made his getaway.

The police were called and, on arrival, discovered a trail of blood, which they followed down Wilson, Short, and Walnut Streets, thinking it would lead them to Broaddus. Instead, that trail had been left by a young man who had been in a room with one of the girls when the excitement started. In making his move for a quick escape, he had jumped through an unopened window. He came from a well-known Lexington family, and the news stories did not name him. He later became a prominent Lexington druggist, whose experience that night left him with a limp which he never discussed.

Meanwhile, Broaddus had gone into hiding at the slaughterhouse on Old Frankfort Pike, across from the Pepper Distillery, but was later persuaded by his father and brother to surrender. He was arrested the evening after the murder and lodged in the county jail. After a hearing, Broaddus' case was held to the grand jury and tried in the next term of court. He was judged not guilty by reason of insanity and sent to the asylum on Fourth Street. He escaped a few weeks later, got out of Kentucky, and took up residence with relatives in Florida. In September of 1914, he committed suicide. Although he was buried in Lexington, the funeral notice did not mention Debbie or the murder.

Debbie, described by many as an extremely beautiful red-haired girl, was twenty-two at the time of her death. She was known in the house as Alice Ely, after having been brought in by her cousin, Emma Harvey, who was also one of Belle's girls. Debbie was an orphan, said to have come from Jackson, Kentucky, and to have been married to a local barber before their breakup, which led to her entering the profession. Between the pages of Belle's old account book is a small lock of red hair, perhaps a remembrance of the unfortunate girl.

After the funeral, Belle and the girls went back to the house, which was closed for the evening. Belle sent to the cellar for a bottle, and the girls sat around the parlor drinking and crying. Each drink brought on more tears, and the girls began to love the memory of Debbie more than they had ever loved the girl herself. After a second bottle had been consumed, Lulu Rose said, with great emotion, "She. . . . She. . . . She gave the best damned ★★★★★★ job on the hill." A new wave of tears streamed forth; and little Fern sobbed, "That's life for you. They never say anything nice about you till you're gone."

The murder of Debbie Harvey at Belle's place was not the first dramatic incident on the hill to receive newspaper coverage. The *Lexington Press* of August 9, 1892, carried the following account of an event which, fortunately, had a less tragic outcome.

He was unfaithful. He transferred his attention to another woman. This made life a blank for her. Six ounces of morphine she swallowed, but her life is saved by the prompt efforts of a physician, and now she and her lover are reconciled and she is glad she didn't die.

Mattie Crabtree is the assumed name of a frail creature, who is an inmate of the guilded palace of shame presided over by Mag Dobbs, 38 Megowan Street.

She is said to be the daughter of ex-Mayor Higgins, of Somerset whose attempt last spring to assault a woman and his indictment by the grand jury now make him a fugitive from justice. He was admitted to bail and forthwith escaped to parts unknown.

Mattie Crabtree is a girl of only about 20 summers and is a very pretty little woman of the brunette type. She went astray less than a year ago and late last winter she came to this city and became an inmate of the house she is now in.

Soon after her arrival she formed the acquaintance of M. J. Kelley, a switchman in the C and O yards, and since then his amorous attentions have been devoted exclusively to her. She became firmly attached to him and Sunday night her heart strings were sorely torn when he passed her by for another of her frail companions.

His infidelity was more than she could endure. Life without his love was a blank and she determined to put an end to her sad existence.

So she came down town early yesterday afternoon and going to the drug store of J. C. Bryant, purchased a six ounce bottle of morphine and returned to her "house".

About half past two she swallowed the entire amount, and a moment after rapidly began to succumb to its soporific influence. Five minutes after, the landlady discovered her condition, and gained from her what she had done.

Dr. J. C. Carrick was summoned at once and applied heroic treatment. The enormous amount of the drug which the girl had swallowed saved her life, for it had a counteracting effect and with prompt medical treatment she was in a few hours rescued from danger.

After recovering she repented her rashness. Her lover repented of his infidelity and last evening both were united by the same bonds of love that have united them for the six months past.

Many felt these unfortunate girls were fair game as the butt of their jokes. One night, four of the town sports were out tearing around in their four-horse sleigh. They decided to go by Belle's place and take the girls out for a ride. When the young men called from the street, the girls quickly put on their coats. Thrilled at the attention and excited at the thought of going riding, they came out and got in. They drove like the wind as the girls squealed and the men urged the horses on. At the first toll gate house on the Paris Pike, the driver whirled the horses rapidly, turning the sleigh over and dumping the whole lot out into the snow. No one was hurt. While the boys were righting the sleigh, they had an inspiration. They climbed into the sleigh and drove away, leaving the girls to walk home.

Jokes such as this seemed to give some men great satisfaction — as though they were showing the women how low their station in life really was. As the girls walked home in the snow, they were reminded once again that they were of little interest except in their role of prostitute.

For some time, Belle had seen the standard she had tried to maintain at her house degraded by other houses on the hill. She had tried to keep the district free of major scandal; now tragedy had struck in her own place, and she was no longer able to hold herself up as an example. At one time, she might have been considered the unofficial mayor of the red light district; but of late, resentment of her success had caused other madams to disregard her warnings that they must operate within the framework set up by the elected officials. Now the sisterhood that had existed among the women was split by envy, and the gulf was widened by the "small house" madams who might have been even a little glad to see that Belle's "palace" was not as invulnerable as they had thought.

In a letter to the editor of the *Leader* a few days after Debbie Harvey's death, a "Citizen" pointed out that, in the preceding ten months, there had been three women murdered on the hill "and two others had recovered from wounds thought to be fatal." The letter adds that two men and one woman from the hill had committed suicide in the same period.

Belle grieved for Debbie, but she also worried about the publicity. Many of the foolish madams thought the hill would go on forever, but Belle still remembered Charles Moore and the circumstances that forced her to leave North Upper Street.

As Meadors' and Jordan's interest in the Brezing collection increased, they began, sometimes individually and sometimes together, to go to see the people still living who had known Belle. These interviews, some on note paper and some retyped by Meadors' wife, give interesting insights into the lives of Belle's old friends and associates.

On a warm August afternoon in 1941, Joe Jordan turned his old car off East Short Street on to the block known as Curley Avenue (formerly East Short Extended). He pulled up in front of 346, a neat little frame house with a fenced yard, and seeing the door open, figured Clara Sayre was home. He killed the engine; and as he got out, he noticed that several of the houses in view already had girls sitting out on the porches. It would be an hour or more before dark and the start of the evening's business. Perhaps they were using their porches, as others around town were used, as the coolest spot to be found on a hot summer day; but he knew they would soon be the showrooms for the activities of the evening.

As he rapped on Clara's screen door, he noticed he was being observed from the other porches. Perhaps the watchers thought he was looking for a woman and didn't know that Clara didn't run a house. When Clara came to the door, she recognized him, although they hadn't seen each other in several years.

Through the screen, Joe told Clara his business. He was getting some information together on Miss Belle and knew the two women had been friends for years. He wondered if Clara would tell him some things to help fill in some gaps. He had tactfully avoided saying anything about the woman having worked for Belle; that would have to come from her. Clara, of course, was aware everyone knew she had started out as one of "Belle's girls," but she thought it considerate that Joe had not mentioned it. She opened the screen door for him as she said, "I don't know what I can tell you that everybody don't already know."

Once inside, and as his eyes became adjusted to the room, he noticed a picture on the wall of a beautiful young girl. "Is that your picture?" he asked. It was as good a starting point as any.

"Yes," she said, "that was made when I was seventeen, about a year after I came to live with Miss Belle."

So quickly had the guard been let down that it surprised the reporter. Perhaps this interview would go better than he had thought.

"You were only sixteen when you went to Belle's?" he asked.

"Yes, I was living with my family in Cincinnati; and one day a peddler came to the door with a pack on his back selling laces, shawls, and stuff. He said he thought I was beautiful, and how would I like to work in Miss Belle Brezing's famous house in Lexington."

Joe didn't say anything, but he thought something must have gone on between the peddler and the girl first or he would not have asked if she wanted to be a prostitute.

"He told me how beautiful it was," Clara went on, "and how much money I could make, and how Miss Belle would help me to get new dresses and everything." Her voice trailed off, and she seemed to be remembering that day so long ago and the peddler as he made his play. "Anyway," she said, "I told him I would like to do it. A few days after I got a telegram, 'Come at once, signed Belle Breezing'; and she wired me a train ticket."

"I guess I was sixteen," the woman continued. "I know it hadn't been long since I quit playing with dolls."

"Was your family's name Sayre?" he asked. He knew the answer, but he wanted to hear it from her.

"No, my right name is Clara Kessler, but I took Eph's name when we were together." Eph was Ephraim Sayre, Jr. His father was nephew and heir to David A. Sayre, an early Lexington banker and founder of Sayre School. In addition to giving Lexington another institution of learning, his other acts of generosity were impressive. It was said he gave over half a million dollars to charities and, having no children, left legacies by name to fifty-six relatives.

Joe remembered Tandy Hughes saying that young Eph stuttered and sometimes had to say "Itsby" to get started again. "I heard Eph stuttered," Joe said.

"Just when he got upset," the woman replied almost defensively. "He didn't do it when we were alone together." She reflected a moment, and Joe waited. "I hadn't been at Miss Belle's long when I met Eph," she said. "We fell for each other, and he didn't want me to be with any other man. I stayed at Miss Belle's, but he paid my board, and I was just his." She went on, "He was sure good to me, took me everywhere with him. Opera House, circus, and on Sunday afternoon we always took a drive in his carriage. Right down Main Street. He didn't care if people knew where I lived or not. He liked me being young and all. He took me in the best stores in town and bought me the pertiest clothes, but he always wanted me to dress like a young girl. He wouldn't let me have anything a woman would wear."

"He wasn't very old when he died, was he?" Joe asked.

"No, just thirty-seven. It didn't seem young to me then, but it does now," she replied with a slight smile.

"What did you do then?"

"Well, I kept on living at Miss Belle's as one of her girls until Clem brought me over here to this house."

"Clem Beachey?" Joe asked.

"Yes, Clem used to come to Belle's a lot; but we never paid much attention to each other until he and his regular girl had a falling out. Then he started coming to see me." Clem was one of the most successful, and prosperous, trotting horse trainers and drivers on the Grand Circuit. "Clem wanted a place to entertain his horse people," she said, "and he asked me if he bought a house would I come and keep it for him. Clem never lost a dime keeping this place," she said.

Joe had heard about Clem Beachey before. As trainer, Clem advised his wealthy patrons about the purchasing of young stock for future racing. During the morning, they would tour the farms, looking at yearlings. In the evenings, he and his prospects would gather at Clara's. There would be plenty to eat and drink; and since Clara knew all the girls and her house was only a short walk from Miss Belle's and other houses in the district, there was no trouble about having a good-looking girl for each male guest. After one of his patrons was in a mellow mood, Clem might say, "You know that bay colt we were looking at this morning at Ernest Featherstone's? He looks like just what we need for two-year-old stakes next year, and I can buy him for you for $15,000.00."

"Go ahead, Clem, and buy him." And Clem no doubt already had an option to buy the colt for $5,000.00.

"I have known him to sell $100,000.00 worth of horses right here in this house during a trot meet," Clara said.

"Tandy Hughes told me you were a fine cook and used to fix some wonderful meals for Clem's customers," Joe said.

"I don't ever remember fixing anything special for old Tandy, but I did put out some fine meals."

"When did Clem die?" Joe asked.

"In 1913. He came in on the circuit that year, and we had planned to get married, and he was going to retire as soon as the meet was over. He bought a big apple orchard in Washington state, and we were going there to live, all new and everything. When he got in, I knew he was sick as soon as I saw him. His color wasn't right. He went to Mt. Clemens, Michigan, and a lot of other places; but they couldn't even find out what was wrong with him. Finally, he just couldn't get up one morning. I called the doctor, but he couldn't help him. The next day they took him out to St. Joseph's Hospital. His family all came, but he died a few days later. His folks were all fine people. One of his sisters was an artist, and a brother was editor of a big horse paper. They didn't say a thing when they found out what Clem left me.

"They took his body back on the Queen and Crescent to Lebanon, Ohio; and I'll never forget how I felt standing out there on Broadway watching that train pull out."

Joe wondered if she had gone to the short service that he had heard was held at the Maxwell Street Presbyterian Church, but he did not ask. "What did you do then?" he asked.

"Well, I never run a house."

This wasn't true; she did have girls until 1917.

"I used to let some rooms to couples who wanted a place to meet in private."

It seemed she was tired of the sad part. After a moment, she smiled and said, "A man and his wife used to both come here. With other people, that is. And neither one knew the other was having dates here. One night they were both here at the same time. So I had to tell her that her husband was here. This woman had a high laugh that anybody could recognize who had ever heard it. So that night I told her, 'You'll have to keep quiet tonight. Your husband is in the room across the hall.' And she kept quiet, too. I knew she could never afford to get after him about being here. But if he heard her laughing, no telling what might have happened. I didn't want any trouble in my house."

Joe began to ask the questions he had in mind when he came there, and Clara seemed happy to oblige him. Prompted, she remembered when the girl who later married Judge John J. Riley came to Belle's. Belle had been to Louisville during the race meeting there and had met a madam from Buffalo, whom she brought home with her for a visit. After the Buffalo woman got back to her house, she was telling her girls what a fine establishment Belle Brezing had at Lexington. One of them expressed a wish to work for Belle, and so it was arranged.

After Judge Riley got crazy about the girl, he moved her out of Belle's house; and they lived together over on Dewees Street, just at the edge of the district. He later married her, and they moved to a better part of town.

Joe knew that several of Belle's girls married men who had met them at the house. In addition to Clara Sayre and the girl who married Judge Riley, one married a Mr. Greenbaum, who owned the distillery at Midway. Another married a prominent Lexington physician. Several others married wealthy landowners whose wives were now no colder in the grave than they had been in bed. These men found the sexual satisfaction obtained with their new wives worth the criticism they received from their neighbors. It was a good deal for both parties. The girls had nice homes, and it was a lot easier to take care of one older man on a very irregular basis than four or more almost every night. The man got a companion and a bed partner who was as different from his first wife as night from day. Most of the girls married men who lived away from Lexington and came here for the running races or the trots. With them, it was not so much of a problem. They would take their new wives back to wherever they lived, and nobody there would know about the girls' past.

Everybody in Lexington knew where Judge Riley had met his wife. It didn't seem to have hurt his popularity at the polls; he kept on winning.

Another of Belle's girls married the owner of a Lexington jewelry store. She joined the church and lived a very respectable life. Everybody knew her history, too; but she was well treated at church.

Clara also told Jordan of her trip to Bell Place, the old mansion now in the center of the Bell Court area.

> One night D. D. Bell was at Miss Belle's, and he got to bragging about what a pretty little girl he had. Then he said, "I tell you! My wife's out of town. Let's go out to the house, and I'll show you my little daughter."
>
> So he called for his carriage, and loaded it up with me and some other girls, and took us out to that big mansion. The little girl was asleep in an upstairs room. So we all tiptoed in and looked at her.

Joe wondered if Clara knew that the little girl grew up to be Clara Bell, perhaps the most popular and sought-after young woman in Lexington society of her day. She married Julius Walsh, a St. Louis millionaire, and later lived at the Plaza in New York City. Jordan thought that some time, when she was in town, he would tell Clara Bell Walsh about the night visitors she had had when she was a baby.

Clara Sayre had bought Miss Belle's bedroom furniture for $1,600.00 at the auction after Belle's death. She told Joe, "A fellow was here yesterday, wanting to buy Miss Belle's bedroom suit, and what do you think he offered for it? $3,000.00."

"Well, it's nice furniture. But $3,000.00 is a lot of money," Joe said. "I guess you sold it to him, didn't you?"

"No, I didn't. I like it. I was with Miss Belle the day she bought it at the Exposition in 1894, and I don't need the money. So I thought I might as well keep it."

Clara told Joe that Belle had once paid Amos Wheeler for a bill she owed with a fine piece of jewelry worth considerably more than the amount due him. On another occasion, she paid an outstanding bill with a large crystal punchbowl. Clara indicated Belle had done this in one of those periods when she had worried about her dwindling funds. Or possibly she was under the influence of the morphine upon which she became more and more dependent.

It was getting dark outside, and Joe could see the evening procession of cars driving around, gawking at the girls on the porches, some drivers looking for a new girl, others building up their courage to stop. He got up and walked over to inspect the picture of Clara now that she had turned on the lamps. How innocent she looked. Eph had wanted to keep her a child, Clem had wanted her for a wife, and she had lost them both. Now she lived in her little house alone with a lifetime of memories that would shock most people.

"When I'm gone, you can have that picture, you like it so much," Clara said, half joking; and Joe assured her he would love to have it. He told her goodby and asked if he could come back again, as he was sure there were other things he would think to ask.

She said, "Any time. I like to talk to somebody about old times."

Joe pulled away from the curb, and Clara went back into the house. As he stopped at the corner before making his turn onto Wilson, a girl across the street hollered, "Honey, over here." As he shifted into second, heading toward North Eastern and Miss Belle's old corner, he could still hear the plaintive call, "Honey. . . . Honey."

At about the same time in 1941, Joe Jordan interviewed Blanche Patterson. Her statements provide further insight into the operation of the hill. At the time of the interview, Blanche was living in a shotgun house on Wilson Street and had only one girl, whose fee was $1.00, of which Blanche received fifty cents. Business was brisk the night he was there, according to Jordan; customers had to pass through the front room in which he and Blanche were talking.

Blanche, whose real name was Mary Jackson, said that her family had lived on Lexington Avenue when she was growing up. She had worked for Bogaert's Jewelers, but started running around with several couples, drinking, and even staying out all night once. She didn't get to work the next morning. When she did appear for work, Bogaert fired her. She then went to Belle's place at Megowan and Wilson, applied, and was accepted. She was then sixteen years old.

Blanche told Jordan that Miss Belle always outfitted her new girls with nice clothes, taking installments out of the money due the girl each week until she was repaid. Blanche, who was an old woman at the time of Jordan's interview, always referred to Belle Brezing as "Miss Belle," and never as simply "Belle." Jordan noted this was also true of Clara Sayre and others who had been among Belle's girls.

After Blanche had been with Belle a short time, she was recognized by a man delivering ice, who lived near her family. He evidently told them where she was, "for they came and got me." However, she went right back at the first opportunity. After that, her family made no further attempt to rescue her.

She said that Miss Belle did not take a percentage of all the money a girl made. She collected $5.00 from the men; or if a man had an account at the house, the $5.00 was charged to him and counted as cash as far as the girl was concerned. At the end of the week, Belle deducted $24.00 ($21.00 for a week's room and board; $1.00 for towels; $1.00 for maid service; and $1.00 for something else, possibly laundry, but Blanche could not recall exactly), plus an installment on account if the girl still owed for clothes or money advanced. The girl received the rest, plus any tips she may have been given. Tips were strictly between the girl and the man. Belle never tried to find out the amount or to claim any part of them. Blanche said the tips were often pretty good, with $10.00 being not an usual amount. "During the trots," she reported, "it was nothing for some of those trotting horse men to slip a $50.00 bill in a girl's stocking, while still downstairs in the parlor, to give them luck the next day at the track."

"Miss Belle never insisted that a girl drink with a customer, if the girl didn't drink," said Blanche. "But she sure had better *order* a drink if a man offered to buy." There were big brass cuspidors placed all around the parlors, and the girls could empty their drinks in them and pretend to be drinking. This was because beer, wine, and liquor were a major source of income for Belle. Beer, then a nickel a bottle everywhere else, was $1.00 a bottle at Belle's; wine sold for $5.00 a bottle.

Blanche was vague when Jordan asked how much a girl could make a week, over and above Belle's deductions. She indicated it varied too much from time to time to say what was average. "A lot of it depended on how hard a girl wanted to work. If she didn't feel like it, she didn't have to hustle." In other words, she was not required to make a play for a man simply because he had come in the downstairs parlors. Even if he asked, she didn't have to take him if she didn't like his looks or didn't like him. She could say she already had a date and was just waiting for the man who had spoken for her for the night. "Some girls hustled a lot harder than others," said Blanche.

Blanche also could not say how much was the most she ever

made in one night, but recalled one time she and another girl had a bet on which one could make the most that night. "I'll never forget that, because she beat me by $1.00. She made $76.00, and I made $75.00, and she won the bet." She wasn't sure that was the most she ever made in one night; she just remembered that because it was so close.

She confirmed what everyone said, that is, that Miss Belle did not permit profanity or dirty talk downstairs. Both customers and girls had to behave like gentlemen and ladies in the parlors. It was also a rule that a girl could not come downstairs after 6:00 in the evening unless she was in evening dress. There was no sitting on the porch, no beckoning out the windows at those passing Miss Belle's. When her girls went downtown, they had to be dressed modestly and behave themselves. A primary rule, of course, was that they must never show recognition of a customer they might happen to see off the premises.

Blanche was later madam of her own house, across the street and further up on the hill from Belle's place. In relating an incident to Jordan, Blanche had said, "That was when I was still at Miss Belle's, before I went to housekeeping for myself." "Going to housekeeping" was a common expression used by those opening their own houses.

After Blanche opened her own place, Joe Keith (who for many years operated Keith's Bar and was well-known as a proprietor of the Golden Horseshoe, a famous watering place across the street from the old Phoenix Hotel in downtown Lexington) said her house at 70 Megowan Street was a half a story above the ground level. She kept the liquor in a locked icebox in the basement. There were windows in the basement high enough for a man to pass through. Blanche kept the keys to the icebox in her pocket. One of the boys would ask Blanche to dance, telling her how good looking she was, distracting her so that he could steal the keys out of her pocket. Then he would slip down to the basement, unlock the icebox, come back up, and dance with her again, putting the keys back in her pocket. The word would be passed around to everyone, including the girls. They would slip down to the basement when Blanche had gone to her room. After a while, Blanche, realizing it was mighty quiet, would start to investigate and find the girls had gotten too drunk to hustle. That was when the smart boys would go out the basement windows. Otherwise, Blanche would not have let them in the next time they showed up at her house and she recognized them.

Mrs. Margaret Egbert told Meadors:

Nell Welch, from up there at Blanche Patterson's, bought her a car. She loaded it up with some of the girls and they went to Nicholasville. They almost burned up the car was so hot, and they heard something clicking and thought the car was in bad shape. They went to the first garage they come to when they got into town, and the only thing that was wrong was the heater was on.

On July 9, 1956, Meadors interviewed Colonel Phil Chinn. The colonel, a well-known horseman, was considered by many to be the best judge of thoroughbred horse flesh of his time. Three of the colonel's stories follow.

Allie Baunta, who was a Boston banker interested in trotting horses, would come to Lexington a couple of weeks before the trots and stay until after the meet was over. He would usually lease Belle's place — lock, stock, barrel, and girls — and entertain his friends there. His lease always ended the day the trots were over, and he must have paid well because Belle had to turn away all of her old regulars for the period of the lease.

One night during such a time, Warren Stoner of Paris, Kentucky, had an oyster feast at the Phoenix Hotel for his friends. He had oyster stew and then fried oysters. "Yes, sir," said the colonel. "He had oyster stew and then fried oysters." As Stoner and his friends imbibed freely while they partook of the shellfish, they began to think of more mundane pleasures. Stoner called Belle and said he was going to bring his friends up for a little while. Miss Belle told Stoner that Allie Baunta had her place leased and that she could not let him in. He was so sure she would change her mind when they got there that he and his guests loaded up in hacks and soon arrived on the hill.

It must have embarrassed Stoner when Belle wouldn't yield, so he and his party went across the street to Mollie Irvine's. Mollie was a black madam, but all the girls in her house were white. Mollie put Stoner and his eight guests in a separate parlor and sent in three girls. When Stoner called her to ask why there were no more girls for his party, Mollie said the rest of the girls were dancing with some additional guests in the dancing room. His embarrassment must have been mounting. He insisted she call the girls and, finally, leased the house with the understanding it would be closed to everyone but him and his guests and that his lease was to run out when Baunta's lease at Belle's did.

Col. Chinn recalled how his father would have the young Phil and several of his friends for dinner at the Phoenix, then give each boy a five dollar bill after the meal and tell them to go up on the hill to see Belle Brezing and get fixed up with a girl. "But if I ever catch you fooling around a nice girl, I'll kill you."

Phil Chinn also had a story as to why Joe Keith never married. Keith's father ran a saloon on the hill; and Joe and his brothers were runners for the old man, taking whiskey to the various houses. Joe fell in love with a girl who was staying at Miss Belle's and wanted to marry her. She told him she would have to talk to Ma and Pa about that. Since she was from up in the mountains, Joe said, "You are figuring on going home, anyhow, so you go on and talk to your folks. I'll get us an apartment fixed up downtown; and when you get back, we will get married and move in." When she got back, Joe met her at the train, planted a big kiss on her, and told her to come on over to the courthouse and they would get a magistrate to marry them.

"No," she said, "I can't do that. I talked to Ma and she said to talk to Pa and he said not to do it."

Joe asked if her people knew where she was living and what she was doing. She admitted that they knew she had a room here in Lexington and that she did entertain men. "Well, why don't they want you to marry me then," asked Joe.

"Pa said," she answered, "that when I married, he thought I ought to marry a man who would raise me socially." This so angered Joe that he decided then and there that he never would get married and he didn't.

Through the years, the people on the hill — prostitutes or blacks — were often the beneficiaries of Belle's generous heart. John Coyne, the old bartender, told Meadors "an awful lot of stuff went out the back door to the poor people of the neighborhood."

Once, when the Protestant Infirmary a block from Megowan had a fire, it was reported they were in need of sheets. Belle called the owner of the Peerless Store on Main Street and bought all the sheets, pillowcases, towels, and washcloths in stock and had them sent to the hospital. When the grateful nurses asked who had been so generous and were told it was Miss Belle Brezing, they became damned ungrateful and refused the gift, saying that it was bought with "tainted money."

Coyne said that "for every bad thing Belle did, she did five hundred good ones."

Pinkie Thomas was one of Belle's girls who later opened her own house, but the two remained close friends over the years. According to Coyne, Pinkie was beautiful and "the talk of the town when she first came to Belle's."

Belle and Pink (as she was called by her friends) went to Cincinnati to the races one day and, along with some ten other folks, drank five bottles of wine. Belle told Pink, "If I get drunk, call for me at the hotel tomorrow; but inquire for Mrs. Kenney, not Brezing." Next afternoon, when Pink got to the races, there was Belle sitting there as fresh as a daisy, with a half pint of whiskey in front of her. So they started off again with another drink. Some of the boys from Lexington came by; and in answer to Belle's question, they said they had gone broke on the first race. Belle gave them some twenty-five or thirty dollars and told them that they could pay her back if they won; if not, they didn't owe her anything.

Pink said a man from Wichita, Kansas, stopped by one day and wanted to go "hoppin'"; so Pink took him around to Belle's. She knew he was a good spender. She sent word up, and Belle came down all dressed up and wearing a handful of diamonds. The trotting horse man ordered a bottle of wine and Belle said, "Duplicate that order." She was always willing to do her share. Belle said, "Looks like we're going to get drunk, don't it?" When Pink and her friend left, he remarked that he had never been treated nicer anywhere.

At the Phoenix Hotel on the night of a presidential election, returns were being received by wire in the lobby. Pink said all the Democrats would shout themselves hoarse when a county went in favor of Cleveland and take the advice of anyone who said, "Let's have another drink." When a county went for Harrison, the Republicans would do the same. About 1:00 a.m. Miss Belle came in. "My, she did look pretty with her tight waist and long dress and the prettiest hat with ostrich plumes on it," Pink said. "When she heard the election was going for Cleveland, she got so excited she took off her pretty hat and threw it on the floor and jumped on it." (Possibly she was thinking of Singerly, who was a friend of Cleveland's.)

Belle was walking past Pink Thomas' one day and remarked she didn't have time to stop. She said she was on her way to the bank. She had a check from Clarence Mackey for $1,500.00, and she was anxious to cash it. On the way back, she stopped in and told Pink, "If I had known I wasn't going to have any trouble cashing it, I would have gotten $2,500.00."

CHAPTER 7

Twilight

In 1917, Belle's world began to come apart. The 1915 closing of the hill had been little more than a scare; but the opposition forces were gathering more strength with the alliance of the anti-vice people, churches, and other citizens. Belle knew her operation would be severely altered, if not entirely closed. But she was also faced with an event which affected her far more than the threat to her business.

Billy Mabon had been ill for some time, suffering with chronic nephritis; and the new year began with the almost certain realization that he would not live long. He died on February 16, 1917.

Billy's body was taken to the home of his sister, Mrs. Morgan, 408 West Third Street. Mrs. Morgan was the widow of Colonel Richard C. Morgan, who fought in the Civil War with his brother, General John Hunt Morgan, the leader of Morgan's Raiders, known as the "Thunderbolt of the Confederacy."

The following notice appeared in *The Lexington Leader* on February 17, 1917.

WILLIAM MABON.

In compliance with a wish relative to the disposition of his remains, expressed before his death, the body of William Mabon, for years auditor and cashier of the Lexington Water Works Company, will be cremated.

The funeral services for Mr. Mabon will be held at the residence of his sister, Mrs. R. C. Morgan, 408 West Third street, Sunday afternoon at 3:30 o'clock. Rev. Thomas B. Roberts, pastor of the Centenary Methodist church, assisted by Right Reverend Lewis W. Burton, will conduct the services. Accompanied by relatives and friends the body will be taken to Cincinnati Monday morning for cremation.

Although Mrs. Morgan probably did not approve of her brother's association with Belle, there is every indication that they remained rather close throughout Billy's life. Neighbors reported that when Billy called on his sister he frequently would be in Belle's well-known carriage, and he would always pull it around to the back of the house in order not to embarrass his sister.

On the evening before the funeral, visitors called at Mrs. Morgan's to pay their respects. After everyone had left, Belle came. Because of her experience when calling at Johnny Cook's unannounced many years before, it is almost certain she came either by invitation of Mrs. Morgan or after having requested her permission. She entered the room where Billy's body lay, and the large doors were closed behind her. She remained there for some time. She did not attend the funeral held at 3:30 on Sunday.

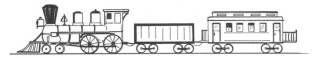

Billy's body was taken on a special railroad car, accompanied by friends and relatives, to Cincinnati, where his remains were cremated.

The young Stoll girls, who were neighbors of Mrs. Morgan's, were fascinated by the story of the cremation since it was a custom new to Lexington. They would go to Mrs. Morgan's home as though paying a social call. When they were seated in the parlor and had engaged in some little conversation, one of the girls would ask for a glass of water. When Mrs. Morgan left the room, the girls would quickly take the urn from the mantel, remove the top, and look in at "poor Mr. Mabon."

The Hunt family and the Morgans are all buried in the Lexington Cemetery in Section C, Lot 12. The Hunt children, grandchildren, and other relatives are buried in graves in a circular arrangement around the large center stone erected when John Wesley Hunt (who was said to have been the first millionaire west of the Alleghanies) and his wife died.

Lexington, situated in the heart of bourbon country, had a saloon on almost every street corner in the late nineteenth century. Many groceries sold whiskey, often by the drink, in addition to their usual staples.

In 1881, there were forty-two saloons within the city limits, which then extended only a few blocks in each direction from the courthouse. Thus, a number of taverns located outside this area were

OUR
FATHER AND MOTHER

JOHN WESLEY HUNT
BORN AUGUST 1773.
DIED AUGUST 21ST 1849.

CATHERINE HUNT
BORN FEBRUARY 1777.
DIED OCTOBER 17TH 1835.

THEIR CHILDREN SLEEP AROUND

Detail of a small portion of the center stone in Hunt Family lot. Certainly the engraved phrase would not have had its present connotation when the stone was erected.

not included in the count. Booze was available seven days a week until May of 1886, when the commission voted to close saloons on Sundays.

Liquor continued to thrive in Lexington; by 1894, there were 110 liquor licenses issued within the city and five more awaiting approval pending investigation. Most of the houses on the hill were licensed.

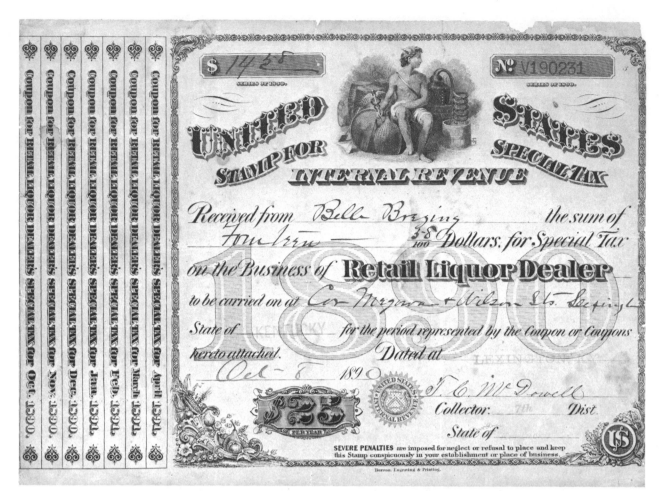

It has been reported that Belle did not open her house on Megowan Street until 1891. It is obvious, however, from the date on the license reproduced above, October 8, 1890, that the house was opened in 1890.

In March of 1895, the count was 200 saloons or groceries selling liquor by the drink. This was a sizable number considering the city limits had remained the same. In November of that year, Judge Jackson in Louisville ruled that "a license to sell liquor was a license to sell it every day of the week." Against mounting opposition in the community, Lexington's saloons reopened on Sundays. State Senator William F. Klair, who had an interest in the health of the distilling industry, was known in Kentucky as the "friend of the saloons," and led the fight to keep them open on the Sabbath.

By law, women were not allowed in any saloon at any time; and police frequently conducted raids to keep these establishments "free of women."

While Belle's place was known for serving the best bourbon, wine, and champagne of all the local bawdy houses, Ed Gleeson's place on Water Street was one of the best-known bars in central Kentucky. It was a place for gentlemen of high breeding and good taste to come and have a civilized drink in the best tradition of such gathering places. Gleeson stocked only one whiskey — twenty-year-old Blackmore, a favorite Kentucky libation at the time.

In February of 1911, the city imposed a limit of one hundred saloons and tried to keep them from opening on Main Street. Licenses were not transferable; once closed, saloons could not be opened again under new management. Still, there were 125 licenses issued in 1914.

That year also saw the raising of the annual liquor license fee and the reduction of the number of licenses. A new law was enacted which divorced the grocery business from the liquor trade.

The crusading ladies of the Women's Christian Temperance Union, together with the local churches, were beginning to exert a great deal of influence in city hall. The enemies of unrestrained liquor sales were starting to win after years of losing. This was accomplished in great part by persuasive women who were still unable to vote.

An ordinance was introduced in 1917 to prohibit the sale of sandwiches or lunch (the long-standing tradition of a "free lunch") to patrons in any saloon. It was defeated, most likely by city fathers who thought such a law was going a bit too far.

As soldiers began to appear in town from Camp Stanley on Versailles Road, new laws quickly followed. A dry zone was set, making it illegal to sell liquor within one-half mile of a military establishment. Also, soldiers were not to be allowed in saloons in Lexington.

Much of the soldiers' training took place at the University of Kentucky; accordingly, six saloons on South Broadway and one on Prall Street near the campus were closed.

Liquor and prostitution both had their adversaries; but as the First World War began, the unification of the reform groups had a great influence. Together, they were able to muster a great deal of public sentiment. Families sending boys off to training camps feared the evils they would be exposed to.

For its October 31, 1917, edition, the Lexington paper dug into its files and quoted from a report submitted by the Vice Commission of Lexington in 1915. The commission was made up of Robert K. Massie, Charles Lee Reynolds, Margaret H. T. Hunt, W. T. Lafferty, John W. Scott, and George S. Shanklin:

THE LIQUOR INTEREST AND COMMERCIALIZED VICE

"Inflamed with liquor and aroused in passion. . . . the men and boys finish the night with the inmates in their rooms."

"The liquor and the dancing are the dangerous stimuli that make it almost certain that every caller will become a customer, even if his sole purpose at first is merely curiosity."

"In practically every house beer is sold. The profit to the madam is enormous. One madam sells on an average $200 worth of beer per week."

"The purpose in the sale of the beer is not simply the money that it alone brings, but the increased business in prostitution, for alcohol impairs the moral resistance. Therefore the first solicitation when customers enter is to purchase liquor."

The paper further quoted the chairman of the Anti-Vice Commission of Seattle, Washington, who said:

"Our great campaign against the social evil was not successful until the saloons were wiped out of Seattle. When the saloons were closed the lewd women of the city, like the Arab, folded their tents and silently stole away."

The October 17, 1917, paper informed readers of the cleanup work being done in other cities by Raymond B. Fosdick, the U. S. Army Training Camp Commissioner. Twenty-two large U. S. cities (they were each named) had wiped out vice in order to protect the soldiers in nearby camps.

When Mayor James C. Rogers was informed by Fosdick that vice conditions were intolerable in Lexington, the mayor seemed quite suprised to learn there were houses of prostitution right here in his city. He immediately called a meeting of the Circuit Judge, Commonwealth Attorney, and Chairman of the Social Hygiene Commission.

The group decided the situation needed a thorough investigation. The mayor wired Fosdick for suggestions. Fosdick wired back, suggesting that a first-class private detective be found in Cincinnati or Cleveland. Rogers called W. A. Pinkerton of the Pinkerton Detective Agency in Chicago, but was informed they "did not handle that class of business." The mayor seemed to be at a loss for a next move. George R. Hunt, Chairman of the Social Hygiene Commission, asked Fosdick to aid in an investigation.

Fosdick, without saying anything to anyone, sent undercover agents to Lexington. Their report (made over three days and reported the same way) was printed in *The Lexington Leader* on Tuesday, October 23, 1917.

REPORT OF INVESTIGATION
BY FEDERAL AGENTS OF
LEXINGTON VICE CONDITIONS

EDITOR'S NOTE—Parts of this report are omitted because of their indecency. The remainder is published with appologies for doing so.

———

Below is the report of an investigation made in Lexington in September by agents of the government detailed to inquire into and report on the moral conditions in the vicinity of Camp Stanley, where soldiers were quartered and made public today by another newspaper.

This investigation was initiated by letters to Chairman Raymond B. Fosdick, of the Commission on Training Activities, by the chairman of the Lexington Commission on Social Hygiene, who requested that the government cooperate with the local authorities and others in their efforts to enforce the local vice ordinances. The report of the secret agents sent to Lexington by Mr. Fosdick follows:

Report of
Investigation.

"Lexington, Ky., September 22, 1917.

Parlor Houses of Prostitution—The following parlor houses of prostitution were visited:

153 Megowan Street—Bell Breezings

Six inmates. Price of house $5. Moerlein's beer sold. Inmates dressed in fancy gowns. No soldiers admitted.

70 Megowan Street—Blanche Pattersons

Five inmates. Price of house $2. Wiedemann's beer sold. Inmates dressed in fancy gowns. Nineteen soldiers were in the house. Eight more soldiers, ossified drunk, were on the stoop of the house waiting to get in.

317 Wilson Street—Hannah McAfee, colored madam

Three white inmates. Price of house $2. One soldier seen here.

322 Wilson Street—Margaret Spears

Four inmates. Price of house $2. Moerlein's beer sold. Inmates dressed in gowns. Three soldiers seen.

519 West Fifth Street—Beatrice Huston

Four inmates. Price of house $5. Moerlein's beer sold. Inmates attired in street dresses—one piece, tight fitting, black garments. Soldiers are not admitted. The madam, a big auburn haired, 40-year-old woman, recently built the house and claims police protection.

In conversation with some of the madams it transpired that at present the grand jury is in session and "we were told to be careful 'till the jury quits." The intimation was strong that the police have full knowledge of all that is going on. They can't help knowing.

By actual count 167 soldiers were seen hanging around East Short street, Wilson street, Megowan street, streets on which the houses of prostitutes are located. The military patrol was there too, but did nothing altho quite a number of soldiers, 16 by actual count, were drunk.

Ice Cream Parlors—Street walkers are using ice cream parlors in their efforts to secure customers. The women simply enter one of these places, order ice cream and remain on exhibition near a window. Soldiers soon enter and join the women, after being openly solicited to do so. Today these parlors were packed with street walkers and soldiers. The "couples" (soldier and prostitute) were kept under observation. After partaking of ice cream, they were seen to leave and enter cheap hotels.

Liquor—Every drunken soldier seen today in Lexington, 16 in all, was on the streets where disorderly houses are located, or in the immediate vicinity. This is undoubtedly due to the fact that in all of the above mentioned parlor houses where soldiers were seen they were drinking. The soldiers but very recently received their pay—hence the large number in the houses paying for a "round" of beer.

Soldiers were seen to consume whisky in but two instances, and then they brought the flasks with them into the houses and used the beer as "chasers."

The saloons were closely watched but none were seen to sell liquor to soldiers.

Soldiers—The streets are thronged with soldiers. They are but youngsters, the majority seeming to be barely out of their teens. On the whole they are well behaved. The intoxicated soldiers apparently keep off the main street.

The Second and Third regiments of Kentucky at Camp Stanley received orders to proceed to Hattiesburg, Miss. Some of the boys about to leave expressed regret at leaving "good old Lexington where a fellow can have fun."

Reports of
Conditions on Sunday.

September 23rd, 1917.
SUNDAY.

Parlor Houses of Prostitution—The following houses of prostitution are additional to those reported upon yesterday. All are running in "full bloom:"

151 Short Street, extended—"Edith"

Two inmates. Price of house $2. Inmates dressed in kimonas. One corporal seen here.

142 Short Street, extended—Clara Sayre.

Three inmates. Price of house $2. Moerlein's beer sold. Inmates dressed in kimonos. Four soldiers seen in the house drinking beer.

326 Wilson Street—Leta Graves.

Three inmates. Price of house $2. Wiedemann's beer sold. Inmates dressed in skirts and waist. Two soldiers seen here drinking beer.

347 Wilson Street—Rose Green, alias Rose Turner.

Two inmates dressed in street clothes. Five soldiers were seen here drinking beer. On Monday, September 24, Rose Green goes to Frankfort to appear before the Federal court. She was raided three weeks ago for selling liquor to soldiers. In spite of this soldiers are being served with beer today. Rose is known as a "bad" woman, having shot a man.

152 Short Street, extended—Annie Williams

"Call" house. Price $5. Soldiers are not wanted.

156 Short Street, extended—Tessie Williams

"Call" house. Price $5. Soldiers are not wanted. Tessie is a sister of Annie Williams.

The following information upon two parlor houses of prostitution reported yesterday:

70 Megowan Street—Blanch Patterson.

This house was kept under observation from 2:10 to 3 p.m. During these fifty minutes, eighteen soldiers entered the place in groups of two and three while six came out.

Liquor—Saloons

Today, Sunday, the saloons are supposed to be closed. The better class saloons are closed, but the cheap places sell all the liquor one can drink or carry away. At least two saloons have Negro solicitors on the streets offering to buy liquor. One Negro, tall brown with stubby mustache and wearing a green soft hat has been soliciting among groups of soldiers, standing at North Limestone and Main streets. The Negro kept remarking "do you want any booze?"

He was seen to accept money from several soldiers and then walk to a saloon on North Limestone where he engaged a big red faced, smooth shaven man in conversation. They entered the side door. The white man appeared to be the manager of the saloon. When the Negro came out he carried several bottles of whisky.

Practically the same procedure was gone thru by a second Negro doing business for another saloon keeper on North Limestone. (Names of the saloon keepers are given in the report but are omitted for the present).

Information is that poker games are carried on in rooms over saloons all along North Limestone under the "club" system.

The Third
Days' Report

Monday, September 24

Eighteen houses of prostitution have already been reported upon and eight new addresses are listed below. This makes a total of 26 houses of prostitution, commercialized and organized that have been visited during the three days' stay in Lexington.

Parlor Houses of Prostitution—The following houses of prostitution, i.e., not reported yesterday or the day before:

181 Colfax Street—Mamie Murphy

Indicted few days ago on disorderly charge, but running just the same. Two inmates. Price of house $2. Moerlein beer sold. Three soldiers seen in house, drinking beer. (She pleaded guilty in July and again yesterday.)

182 Colfax Street—Emma Strange

Indicted few days ago on disorderly charge but running just the same. Two inmates. Price $2. Wiedemann's beer sold. One soldier seen in this house, drinking beer. (Pleaded guilty yesterday).

Twenty-six houses of prostitution reported upon have over 100 inmates.

The number of streetwalkers is about 40.

Streets—Eleven actual solicitations took place to go to eight different places as follows:

Liquor Saloons—The saloons are paying very little attention to the federal law prohibiting the sale of liquors to soldiers. North Limestone street from Main street to Short street, a short block, has nine saloons. Several of them sell liquor to soldiers.

In front of one three soldiers were seen almost helpless from drink. They were unable to walk and were bundled into a Negro hack driver's cab by other soldiers and driven away.

Two soldiers were seen to come from another saloon on North Limestone.

The report didn't seem to surprise anyone but the city officials, who tried to bluff it out. Mayor Rogers revealed that he had hired two men from the Metropolitan Detective Agency in Cincinnati and that their report showed "that conditions were nothing like those reported by the government operatives." Police Chief Jere J. Reagan (forty-three years on the force, fifteen as chief) stated for the papers: "If there are any disorderly houses in operation in Lexington, they are here without my knowledge and consent." Judge John J. Riley had no comment, but said he might at election time (he was up for reelection in November).

In politics, the best defense is to point your finger at someone else; and the heat was on. Time to save your own skin.

Arrangements were made for a meeting of the irate citizens, to be held at the Lexington Opera House, the only space available for what promised to be a large turnout on October 29, 1917.

The mayor took the platform at the meeting and said, in part, "If Police Chief Reagan has not cleaned up vice conditions by November 15th, I will introduce him to his successor."

Headlines on November 4th read: "CHIEF REAGAN, SMARTING UNDER CRITICISM, RESIGNS."

Reagan said, in part, that when arrests were made and the women arraigned in police court the charges were dismissed. In one instance, the policeman making the arrest was fined $50.00 and costs and the accused woman allowed to go free in the police court.

Reagan was replaced by Police Captain James Egan, who had sixteen years on the force.

Again Judge Riley, friend of the prostitutes, had "no comment."

By this time, everbody but the dogcatcher had gotten on the bandwagon: the Woman's Club, the Y.M.C.A., members of the Council of the Board of Commerce, members of the University Council of Deans, the presidents of both universities, the Ministerial Union, the W.C.T.U., all the churches, and the new Health and Vice Squad.

Since the 19th Amendment (which gave women the right to vote) had not been ratified and they, therefore, did not have political clout, the women enlisted the aid of their children in their campaign

against the evils of liquor. Children's books, such as *The Little Folks'
Speaker or Songs and Rhymes for Jolly Times*, were employed to impress the children with the evils of drink. The following excerpts
from this book are samples of what was supposed to be entertainment for the children.

WHEN WE ARE OLD ENOUGH TO VOTE.
Tune:—Yankee Doodle.

> When we are old enough to vote,
>   We'll make a great commotion;
> We'll sweep the land of whisky clean
>   From ocean unto ocean.
>
> "Old Alcohol" will have to fall
>   From his exalted station;
> We'll smite him right, we'll smite him left,
>   And drive him from the nation.

THE Y. U. AND I.

> Kind friends, I will tell you the reason and why
> So many young ladies are joining the "Y."
> The girls of to-day have true cause to think
> That boys should be warned against taking a drink.
>
> For we cannot deny that the boys of to-day
> From the temperance path are going astray;
> A cloud of suspicion hangs over them all,
> For the gayest and proudest are likely to fall.
>
> I will come to the front at the temperance call,
> 'Tis a labor of love intended for all;
> By aiding the Y in their glorious mission,
> The Y, U and I may enjoy prohibition.

Father Punch, a respected local priest, was quoted in an editorial
on October 30, 1917:

> Father Punch hit the nail on the head at the anti-vice meeting
> last night when he said that the law would be enforced in Lexington
> when the people wanted it enforced, and not before.
>
> He did not attempt to excuse official inefficiency or wilful fail-
> ure to enforce the law, but he insisted that upon each individual
> citizen rested the duty, first to keep himself and his household clean
> and then to exercise himself positively about the morals of his
> neighborhood and his town.
>
> Father Punch said he had attended five trials in the police court
> where defendants were charged with keeping disorderly houses. In
> all five of the cases, said he, the evidence of guilt appeared to be
> conclusive but there was an apparent failure of justice in each in-
> stance. Judge Riley dismissed two of the defendants and juries
> brought in verdict of acquittal in the others. Father Punch is too
> intelligent and candid a man either to misunderstand the meaning of
> such travesties or to misrepresent the facts.

Belle was a sensible woman, and she knew the handwriting was on the wall. She had weathered other storms and stayed open, but this was different. Having been indicted by grand juries and cited to court more times than she could remember, she had always paid out. Now those who had protected her were in no position to come to her aid. If she were arrested, the public outcry might carry her to jail, where she had never been.

Billy was gone, and there was no one to turn to for advice.

Many of her regular customers, afraid they would be in the house when a surprise raid was made, stayed away.

After days of worry, she rang the bell. When Pearl came to the room, Belle told her the house would soon be closed. The two women sat through the afternoon, discussing what had to be done. First, the girls would be given some money and sent away. Belle, Pearl, one servant, and possibly a cook would remain to live alone in a house that had been home for so many over the past decades.

Pearl, hoping against hope, said she had talked with Blanche on the street and that she was sure the war would be over soon, the soldiers would be gone from the town, and things would be back to normal. Belle knew it would never be as it once was, and she wouldn't have it any other way.

The girls in the district began to scatter. Some went to Louisville, some to Cincinnati, and still others to areas the Army wasn't interested in. Lexington opened a House of Mercy to take in the fallen flowers and help them to "find a new way of life."

All the charges leveled against Judge Riley did not affect the election; he won with 3,081 votes against the reform candidate who garnered only 1,491.

A few of the smaller houses never completely closed, but their madams feared a stranger at the door; and no soldiers were admitted. Most places turned into room-letting establishments, where a man could make his own arrangements to meet a woman without fear of being caught.

Belle would have none of it. If she couldn't have parties, serve champagne, have the best-looking young girls, and be wide open, it was over as far as she was concerned.

And so the lights in the front of the house were never turned on at night, and a sign was put in the windows: Private Residence. When an old customer came to the door, the bell was not answered.

After over thirty years, the hill was quiet.

The old phone number (951) was changed, and Belle enjoyed the quiet an unlisted number afforded. Blanche Patterson gave up her phone (1691), but had it reinstated in 1934 (Ashland 7922), dropping it again a few years later when the kids thought it great fun to call her at all hours.

Obsessed with the quiet, Pearl began to drink; and when all the bottles in the basement were empty, she started drinking moonshine. Years later, Belle told her cook to "Stay away from shine, that's what killed Pearl." But regardless of her nips, Pearl looked after Belle; and although each had only the other for companionship and they were close friends, Pearl always said "Miss Belle."

After Belle sold her horses and carriage to Mr. Smiley at the livery stable, she took a hack if she had somewhere to go. Occasionally she walked to town, but soon she found it easier to stay in the house and have whatever she needed delivered to her.

Belle's addiction increased; and after the Harrison Act of 1914, Dr. Nevitt had obtained permission from the narcotic inspector to prescribe whatever she needed as an "incurable." The delivery boy from a nearby drugstore, who is now a prominent local attorney, recalls that when he would deliver Belle's "prescription" (only two blocks away), he always received a dollar tip. Other deliveries made around town yielded only a dime, no matter how far he had to pedal, and sometimes not even that.

After the Armistice was signed in 1918, the military installations around Lexington closed. The federal government had no further interest in the sins of Lexington. Slowly, the smaller houses on the hill began to reopen.

The police, who had always considered prostitution to be inevitable, took little interest in the houses as they again began the old trade. At first, everything was rather quiet; but as the madams found they were no longer harassed, they became bolder. The girls who had fallen for that great line, "I'm going to cross the big pond, and I may be dead by this time next month," found they could sell what they had been giving away. There was a lot more comfort in a house than in the back of one of Mr. Ford's "Model T's." Many came from the hills of eastern Kentucky and West Virginia; among men in speakeasies an often-heard one-liner was, "I never met a whore who wasn't from West Virgina."

Belle never reopened. She was fast approaching sixty, and she didn't need the money. She often said that the amateurs had put her out of business. "All you need now is an automobile and a pint of whiskey," she said. Belle and Pearl lived in the big house with a few servants and seldom ventured out.

Some houses remained as "call houses" where no girls stayed on a regular basis. The madam had a list of girls who would come when called. Some were working girls, who would come only for an out-of-town man who wouldn't know them; others were wives whose husbands traveled or who were unhappy in their marriages. The old madams got good money for the rooms and for keeping their mouths shut. Often unhappy wives were married to equally unhappy husbands, and either could be found at different times using a room on the hill; and on at least one occasion, as reported by Clara Sayre, both husband and wife showed up on the same night.

Most of the houses that kept girls charged a dollar. Whiskey was scarce, and the beer was usually homebrew; neither was the moneymaker of the old days. A few girls tried for an extra dollar, but the competition was too great. A man would just move on and get a price at the next house. Soon, a buck was "standard fee"; and that's all a man expected to pay for the few minutes allowed him.

"Hurry up, honey, the old lady will be raisin' hell with me."

Knock, knock. "What are you all doing in there? Your time is up."

Of that dollar fee, the madam received fifty cents. Girls could not afford to dress very well on such meager incomes, no longer were they dressed as their sisters of a few years earlier had been. The days of the big spender were gone on the hill, and most of the girls wore something that came off and went on easily.

Some of the boys newly returned from France had found unique variations in entertainment; and charges were altered as they were accommodated. Usually, the charge was based on what the traffic would bear.

A black family by the name of Murphy had once occupied the house next to Belle's on Megowan Street. Their son had distinguished himself as the jockey who rode three Derby winners. Now the house was occupied by a woman reportedly of great talent. The word around town was that, for a $5.00 fee, she would give a trip around the world. An introduction to sex as performed in the various capitals around the globe. Most of the young men turned down this excursion, silently fearing they would not hold up under such prolonged travel and, faltering, would be left in some strange place like Istanbul. Such orgies were for men tired from years of dissipation, who didn't know how to get off the merry-go-round.

As the girls were no longer as selective, venereal disease was spread; and they were required to visit the Department of Health each Monday morning for an examination. Although they considered this harassment by the city, it did help business on Monday night. Many men who were afraid of what they might catch figured Monday to be the safest night to go up on the hill.

After "Pick" Norton's death in 1901, Belle had helped her sister when money was needed; but it was not until after Belle had closed her house and Hester's children were grown that they saw much of each other. Belle never went to see Hester at her home on West Fourth Street or later on Maryland Avenue, but Hester would often visit Belle. Perhaps Hester's neighbors did not know the relationship between the two women, and Belle thought it best not to embarrass her half-sister.

By 1920, Hester's sons had gone from Lexington, one to become an actor in Vancouver, and the other to work for a time in Cincinnati before moving to join his brother.

Hester was often at Belle's and stayed with her younger sister after ill health made it impossible for her to live alone. She died March 1, 1926, and is buried in Belle's lot in Calvary Cemetery.

The nature of their private conversations is not known, but it is interesting to speculate on what they had to say about their early childhood: George Brezing, William McMeekin, Johnny Cook's death, and Dionesio Mucci. They had meant so much to each other as children and had drifted so far apart in their adult lives. Now, once more, they were together as the final acts were playing out.

On August 29, 1926, after a lingering illness, Pearl died of ovarian cancer and, Belle said, drinking shine. Although Pearl was forty-three, Belle cared for her during her last illness as though she were a child.

Pearl's obituary in *The Lexington Leader* said she was buried in the "family lot." Indeed, she was, in the lot Belle had purchased in 1886; it is there, next to Belle and her mother, Sarah McMeekin, that her remains rest. She was, even if not by blood, very much a part of the family.

In addition to Sarah, Belle's mother, Hester, and Pearl, there were other burials in the lot Belle bought in Calvary Cemetery.

Rebecca Hall, who died December 1, 1887, at the St. Joseph Hospital, is not listed in city directories and probably was a prostitute under an assumed name. There was no obituary in the newspapers at the time of her death. Probably, she was a girl Belle felt sorry for.

Sarah Denney, who was fifty-five when she died January 13, 1929, of pneumonia at St. Joseph Hospital, was from Lancaster, Kentucky. Again, there is no further record under this name.

Simmie Culton, who died of tuberculosis on May 11, 1938, was said to have been the son of "Big Tit Lil" Davidson, a well-known prostitute from the hill. She was one of Belle's girls before going to housekeeping for herself on Wilson Street. Again, Belle's soft heart was touched; she took Simmie into her home in the last stages of his illness.

I talked to an old gentleman who remembered Simmie Culton. He told me Simmie was a "very bad character." To impress me with just how lowly Simmie was, he said, "Mrs. Hughes would never allow him in her stag line." The implication was that nothing more need be said. It seems Mrs. Tandy Hughes taught dancing to young ladies of Lexington in the period just after World War I, and every Saturday night she had a dance at the Phoenix Hotel. Young men would go there to dance with Mrs. Hughes' students, thereby giving the girls more practical experience than classroom instruction allowed. Simmie was considered the best dancer in town; the gentleman said, "He was always picked for the 'ladies' choice' dance at the Pyramid Club, but Mrs. Hughes sure wouldn't let him around her girls!"

On occasion, a woman down on her luck would come and plead with Belle to let her stay at the old house. Belle, perhaps remembering that Christmas Eve in 1879, would consent to let the girl use one of the first floor rooms facing Wilson Street. Soon the word got out that Belle was a soft touch.

The woman would sit by the window and motion to the cars that passed. If she attracted someone, she would let him in the old "family entrance" door. When Belle found out that such men frequently tried to wander about the house, she put a stop to it. She gave the girl some money and sent her on her way. After a few such experiences, Belle stopped receiving anyone and stayed confined to her private quarters on the second floor.

She did not want to see anyone. There was nothing of the past she wanted to discuss. Now that she was in the twilight of her life, everything that she wanted to talk about was already said. The rest she kept inside.

As time passed, Belle seemed oblivious to the action on the street outside her home. She often sat on the sunporch at night and read by the light of an old lamp with a tattered, disheveled, beaded shade. She covered the afternoon newspaper front to back. She had lived in Lexington all her life and knew just about everyone in town, many of the men personally. She read about people whose names brought back memories from the past. Most evenings, she finished with one of the old books she had purchased or been given years before, but never seemed to have had enough time for. The last thing at night, she read her Bible.

She had spent years in reading and had expanded her knowledge. She had outgrown the girls who had worked for her; the few who came by to see the old madam had nothing in common with this little bird of a woman. There had been a time they could laugh and joke together, but Belle no longer had any interest in the lifestyle they had all once shared.

At Christmas time, Belle would have her maid keep an eye out for the paperboy. When he came by, he would be invited into the parlor. "Sit down. Miss Belle wants to see you." Belle would soon come down the big staircase in her dressing gown, a wrapped package in her hand. She would give it to the boy, then sit and talk for a few minutes, just as an interested aunt would talk to a nephew whom she hasn't seen in a while. Kelley Rogers, a Lexington attorney who was one of her paperboys, still has the last present she gave him: a Churchill Weavers handwoven scarf.

Time took its toll on the old house at 59 Megowan. The street name had been changed and changed again. Now, Belle's house was on North Eastern Avenue; the street number was 153. The white paint put on in 1895 was long gone, peeled away by the hot summer suns and the freezing rains of winter. It was easy to see the change in the brick pattern that Belle had once considered so unsightly. Slowly, year by year, trumpet vines worked to reach the topmost floor.

In 1930, the man who was compiling information for the city directory found the yard grown up in weeds and paper trees. Sections of the iron fence had fallen down. He reported 153 North Eastern Avenue as vacant.

When a downspout fell on the south side of the house, it was like the philosopher's tree in the forest: It made no sound, for there was no one there to hear it. Neither Belle nor her maid ever went into the rooms on that side of the big house, and she had not been in the yard in years. When it rained, the water poured down the side of the house. Moss grew where the moisture stayed even in the hot summer when the rains were infrequent. Eventually, the mortar fell away. When bricks began to tumble to the ground, a large section of the wall pulled away from the rest of the house.

Fearful for the safety of their children who often played in the side yard, the neighbor women reported the condition to Jim Shea, the building inspector. Shea told Belle the wall would need extensive repair; if not, the entire house would have to come down.

Belle no longer needed the big house. She was frequently alone there and always alone at night when Emma Parker, the maid, returned to the little house at 349 Wilson Street where she lived with her sister, Susie Reed. It would be easier for Belle to fix up the house at 151 Dewees Street that she had bought in 1888 and move there.

When repairs were started on the Dewees Street property and Belle's plan was revealed, the colored neighbors objected. They did not want this white woman with her scarlet reputation in their area. Things were different than they had been in the last century when prostitution had come to their community and they had been unable to stop it. Many were now registered voters, and the politicians were more attentive to their requests. They went to city hall to protest.

The city manager knew there were no legal grounds to keep Belle from occupying the house; but hoping to settle the matter amicably, he sent old Mrs. Egbert to see Belle. Margaret Egbert knew Belle, as she did most of the women who had occupied the hill in the many years she had been the only woman on the police force. Since she also knew that Belle usually did what she set her mind to, she had little hope of succeeding in her mission.

Emma answered the door, ushered Mrs. Egbert into the front parlor, and went to tell Miss Belle who was there. As the policewoman waited, she looked at the large furniture and tall pier mirrors and was struck by the sheer volume of the furnishings. She conceived a plan.

Meanwhile, upstairs, Belle received the news of the visitor, whose presence in the house would have meant trouble in the old days. Now Belle assumed someone wanted a donation for something or other. Normally, she would have gone downstairs to receive a visitor; but it gave her some small satisfaction to have the policewoman climb the stairs. When Mrs. Egbert came into Belle's room, she found the old madam propped up in bed, reading her Bible.

For years the two women had been on opposite sides of the law. Mrs. Egbert had been strict with the women on the hill when she found a transgression she could move on, but she had always been fair. She had once sent Rosie Green to the penitentiary for bootlegging, but Rosie held no grudge. After her release, she had frequently spoken with Margaret Egbert when they met on the street. The women on the hill knew there had to be law, and Mrs. Egbert had turned down many opportunities to be "bought off." This earned for her a respect not given to the policemen and politicians who frequently had their hands out.

Belle received her guest cordially and indicated a chair as the two exchanged small pleasantries worthy of ladies of some social standing. Soon Mrs. Egbert got around to the business that had brought her there, but she cleverly avoided mentioning that city hall had sent her to try to stop Belle from moving onto Dewees. Instead, she said she had heard Belle planned to move into the little house and had wondered what she would do with all her furniture. Certainly, very little of it would fit in the small rooms on Dewees. "You sure couldn't use this big bedroom suit," she said.

Belle had not seen the little house for some time; suddenly, she realized Mrs. Egbert was right. She thought of all the fine furniture she had been so proud of when she bought it. She could think of nothing, except the furniture in the "girls'" rooms, that she would be willing to part with. She knew she couldn't see someone else take away her beautiful bed, with its matching dresser, armoire, and other pieces. "You're right," she said. "I don't know what I was thinking of."

Mrs. Egbert soon took her leave. It was only a few days later that the men started rebuilding the section of the wall at a cost of several thousand dollars.

CHAPTER 8

Deepening Shadows

When the need for more morphine became too great, Dr. Nevitt would take her, under cover of darkness, to his clinic and slowly begin the torture of reducing her dosage. This was the bad time. In the dimly-lit room, with a small bulb offering the only illumination, the days blended with the nights. Time lost its measure. It was forever twilight, that saddest of all times, when even the most solid of forms lose their shape and can be identified only with deep concentration.

Faces and voices from the past drifted through a never-ending nightmare. Debbie died again at the hands of Broaddus. Sutphin and Sharp played with the little gun. Graves long grown over with the "benediction of grass" opened anew.

She was in this bare room because she had allowed herself an extra amount of the drug so that she might change, in her mind, past events. A young Johnny Cook came again to the back gate. In this imaginary script, written and rehearsed in her mind so many times, there was no gun. That awful day was blotted out, and she and Johnny made a new life together that went on and on in total happiness. Sometimes she could trick her mind into believing Daisy was normal. Belle saw her daughter married to a wealthy man and standing in the town untarnished. Other dreams made Johnny Cook, or Willie Sutphin, her own husband. But then these ghost faces faded and changed, and she saw the handsome face of Billy Mabon or the kindly smile of Singerly. She knew she should not have increased her dose, but anything was better than facing up to the way fate had played its hand. Her lack of control had brought her again to this prison of a room.

Each time she returned home from Nevitt's sanitarium, she resolved to hold her dosage down to the level she had reached under the doctor's care. But always the faces of the past would reappear, and she would blot them out with her needle.

In the same way boys fall in love with their school teachers, there had been those who thought they loved this woman who gave them their first sexual awakening. Now in old age, she could remember but a few of the young ones. The boy who laughed and sang and was so exuberant with youth was almost captured in her mind's eye. But was he the handsome blond boy or was he the dark-haired boy with wide shoulders, suntanned to his waist. Before she could fix him clearly in her mind, he faded; and some unpleasantness captured her thoughts.

The older men, yearning for affection, who translated the want into desire, then to sex, and found no satisfaction in finding satisfaction. The men who were frustrated, not sure why they came there, hating both themselves and her when they left. She had seen it in their faces and felt sorry for them.

It was all there in the melting pot of her never-resting mind. Occasionally, pleasant thoughts bubbled momentarily to the surface; but usually the molten accumulation of her memory would not allow a pleasant thought to linger.

Before she retired for the night, Belle would often stand by the side window in the darkness and gaze out at the street below. She saw young men bolstering their courage as they prepared to do what they'd been told they dare not. She would say almost aloud, "That's just how your fathers and grandfathers acted." Occasionally, she would see an older man hurrying from shadow to shadow to avoid recognition. Some she knew. Silently, she asked, "Old fool, why didn't you quit when I did? Your answer isn't on the hill."

Then she would turn to her bed, letting the mellow sensation from her last injection creep across her mind, shutting out all the unpleasant memories. Hopefully, in their place would come a void and blissful, dreamless sleep.

Downstairs, the moths would be busily eating away at the faded oriental rugs; and the mice would scurry about looking for crumbs left by Emma Parker as she hurriedly fixed anything Belle thought she wanted to eat. Usually, the mice ate more than Belle, as she found no appetite for what she thought she wanted an hour before. She found some small solace in drugs and books. She had nothing more.

McFarland at the bank had her power of attorney and sent the money for Daisy May's care. When he saw the checking account was getting low, he would go to her lock box and take out whatever he thought best, selling stocks, bonds, or jewelry, and depositing the proceeds in her account. The Lexington City National Bank would accept checks on the account signed "Belle Brezing," "Belle Breezing," or "Mrs. J. B. Kenney."

She received a small amount of rent from John W. Stoll, who collected for her on the house on Dewees Street. All the other rental property had been disposed of. McFarland never sold her bank stock; after all, it did pay a dividend; diamonds didn't. It is doubtful that Belle, who had always paid her own way, knew the banker had pled poverty and gotten a reduced rate from St. Joseph's Retreat, where Daisy May was kept.

Belle stayed in her small apartment and saw only McFarland, Dr. Nevitt, and, of course, Emma Parker. On one rare occasion, she had Nevitt contact the University of Kentucky and offer them any books they might want from her collection. Dr. Thomas D. Clark, Samuel M. Wilson, William H. Townsend, and J. Winston Coleman, Jr., went out to the big old house on North Eastern Avenue.

Bill Townsend described Belle on that occasion in the late 1930's:

> Presently "Miss Belle" came down, a thin, bent, white-haired old woman, but with strikingly serene features, gentle and refined in speech and manner. She wore a beautiful kimono of black, watered silk, with pink bedroom slippers on her unusually small feet.

Coleman later told me she seemed highly refined, quiet, and well-spoken. Had he not known who she was and met her under other circumstances, he said he would have assumed her to be the widow of some prominent doctor or lawyer, a well-educated woman who had lived all her life in the highest class of society.

Belle offered them any of the books they wanted; included were first editions of several well-known works. Townsend acquired on this visit the little red journal of Belle's accounts in 1882–1883. (The acquisition was made without the old lady's knowledge.)

In 1938, Dr. Nevitt diagnosed the pain Belle had been suffering as cancer of the uterus, the prostitute's grim reaper. It had killed Pearl, Belle's mother, and several of the girls.

It is doubtful she felt she had been as wicked as the town believed; but knowing her life had been far from pure, she confessed her sins to a priest and felt some of the comfort of forgiveness. Blessed are the pure in heart.

Finally, in early 1940, she was confined to her bed, cared for by Emma, who prepared what little food Belle was able to eat. The servant had been instructed by McFarland that no one was to be admitted to the house, and even Clara Sayre and Blanche Patterson were turned away. Dr. Nevitt was called several times a day to minister to his long-time patient, and her daily dose of morphine was increased. Slowly it reached twenty-five grains. But still it did not relieve her pain.

She was moved to the first floor in the room back of the stairs where, in the old days, she sat watching the front and side doors as she read. She was hardly aware of her surroundings. The room was a dismal place for the woman who had loved her fine furnishings. In an attempt to give some comfort to the frail little body, two mattresses had been placed on the old Victorian bed with a high walnut headboard. There were no curtains at the window, and the inside shutters were kept closed. A bentwood chair, an old round-top trunk, a marble top dresser, and a small oak desk, which held the telephone, constituted the only other furnishings in the small room. There was no rug on the floor, and a bare overhead light suspended from the ceiling supplied the only illumination. The end was near; hopefully, it didn't matter to her where she was.

Few people knew of her condition. For years the only glimpses of her had been at night when she read on the sunporch. For the most part, her books had been the classics. Poe and his raven, Stevenson's adventures. Mark Twain was in her collection, and it is interesting to speculate on how she related to Becky Thatcher and the others who had childhoods so different from her own. She had read the romantic tales of John Fox, Jr., and the beautiful words of James Lane Allen and other Kentucky authors whom she may even have known in the old days.

Emma Parker didn't like the long hours alone in the big house with this dying woman; and she made frequent calls to Dr. Nevitt, often thinking the frail little thing in the big bed was dying or already dead. Sometimes the doctor would make as many as five trips

Photograph made two days after Belle's death of the bed she died in.

to the house in one day, but there was hardly enough flesh on the tiny bones to receive the morphine and nothing more he could do.

Nevitt said later that, in the years she was his patient, Belle never discussed her early life or the business that had flourished in the big house. She knew the doctor came from a different world and could never understand the life she had led. Their friendly conversations had always been about literature, the weather, and current news — the same small talk the doctor had with other elderly patients whose cultural backgrounds were similar to those of the women in his own family. It was almost impossible to picture this tiny lady, who could intelligently discuss the works of Shakespeare and Dante and the poetry of Keats and Shelley, as a painted whore bringing a man to the room upstairs. A man who is finally hanged after ten years in prison awaiting the outcome of all of his appeals is usually not the same man who committed the crime; Belle was certainly no longer the prostitute or madam of the old days.

When the doctor suggested she go to the hospital where she could be better cared for, she flatly refused, remembering how the sister at St. Joseph's had treated her when she had gone to see one of her girls who was dying. She remembered being rejected when she had sent sheets and towels to the infirmary after the fire. No, she would die here in her own home. At least, as far as possible, she was still in control of her surroundings; she was not on someone else's ground.

Finally, as Nevitt increased her morphine dosage, it reached thirty grains a day, a tremendous dose for so small a person, even a long-time addict.

Through the hot nights of July, Belle lay more dead than alive. Emma would raise the old woman's head and give her sips of tea and occasionally persuade her to eat small bites of toast. This and water were all she took. Cloths were kept in a pan of ice water beside her bed to place on her forehead when she was especially restless.

On Saturday, August 10th, she slipped into a coma. There was no more need for the morphine. At last, her brain no longer told her of her pain.

Late that night, Dr. Nevitt called St. Peter's and asked for someone to come to give her the last rites of the church. Father Kline came; and when he entered her room, she was turned toward the wall. He thought he was looking at a small child. Her body had wasted away until she weighed less than seventy pounds.

The doctor stayed that night. Although there was nothing he could do, he felt a certain affection for the old woman who had been his patient for so many years.

It had been a sweltering ninety-three degrees that day, and there was little relief through the night. As the hours passed, he heard voices in the dark street as sleepless people came to their yards seeking a breath of air and children were placed on pallets on the porches. Every hour, he thought Belle would slip away; but the heart that had been hurt so often through the years continued its slow, faint beat. Finally, as the first light came into the eastern sky, the doctor, with his finger on her pulse, looked at his watch. It was 4:30 on Sunday morning, August 11, 1940. Belle Brezing was dead.

Dr. Nevitt called the funeral home. Belle had told McFarland weeks before that Baker Funeral Home, and no one else, was to bury her.

As soon as her body was taken from the house, the doctor left, telling Emma she could go home. There was no use calling McFarland so early; he would have some breakfast first and then call.

The banker, immediately on getting word, called the funeral home and made the arrangements. Casket closed, no visitation, no funeral, and burial as quickly as possible.

The newspaper was not informed of the death (the undertaker would normally have called in the information), and there was nothing about Belle's death in the Monday morning *Herald*. A concerted effort was made to bury the old madam before word of her death leaked out. It is said there was fear the funeral home and grave site would be crowded with undesirables. Presumably they meant her "girls" or, perhaps, curiosity-seekers.

The first thing Monday morning the men were put to work digging the grave beside that of Belle's mother. Father Kline was called to conduct a short service at the grave, and a car was sent to pick him up at St. Peter's. There was no mass; the plan was to get the burial over with as soon as possible and without attracting attention.

C. A. Baker, Fred Baker, and Rodgers Baker (father, son, and grandson) and John Anglin, an employee from the funeral home, were the casketbearers. The hearse left Baker's on South Limestone Street a little before 2:00 p.m. and turned west on Main Street. None of the funeral home employees who were along to carry the body to the grave realized the significance as they drove past the old Mary Todd Lincoln house where their dead passenger had gone to work for Jennie Hill while still in her teens. On past the Barnett house where Daisy May had lived in her infancy and early childhood. Past the house where Belle had spent her own early childhood, the building where George Brezing had operated his store. Past old No. 2 School where Belle's heart had been broken by the children. Past where Mucci had lived and run his hide yard and where Belle had lost her virginity. Past the house where her mother had died and she had been locked out on that rainy spring day sixty-five years before. All the living, the heartaches, and the sadness — in a mere two blocks. Just before they turned left into Calvary Cemetery, they passed Johnny Cook's grave, the small stone visible from the road; but there was no one among them old enough to remember the story of his mysterious death.

They pulled up at the open grave just beside the cemetery lane and, with little trouble, placed the box with its small contents on the straps.

Emma Parker was the only mourner as Father Kline started reading the service. Shortly, two white women walked slowly down the drive, but remained some little distance from the grave as though they knew they were not wanted. Young Baker said he was told they were girls who had worked for the madam (probably Clara Sayre and Blanche Patterson, who would both have come if they had found out about the hurried burial). Neither McFarland nor Dr. Nevitt was there, and there were no flowers. If every person in the town who had been the beneficiary of Belle's charity and generosity had

*John Andrew, son of P. &
Barbra Cook.*

come, it would have been one of the largest funerals the town had
ever seen.

As the Baker employees, the priest, Emma, and the two white
women left, the workmen came to fill the hole there beside the big
stone Belle had erected in 1886. On the side facing the new grave,
words etched over half a century before:

Blessed are the Pure in Heart

Several hours after the burial, the afternoon paper appeared on
the streets with a small notice.

Bell Breazing Dead
Funeral services and burial were to be held at 2 o'clock this afternoon for Bell Breazing, who died at 4:30 o'clock Sunday morning at her home at Wilson· street and North Eastern avenue.

She is survived by one daughter, Daisy Kenney, of Dearborn, Mich.

That same afternoon, McFarland dismissed Emma Parker and hired Bill McCowan to guard the house. He also called Sam Downing to arrange for an auction as soon as possible. He contacted St. Joseph's Retreat to inform them of Belle's death (using the name of Mrs. J. B. Kenney) and advised them that a committee should be appointed to approve the sale and receive the residue of the estate in Daisy May's name.

As word spread during the afternoon that Belle was dead and buried, the news became the leading topic of conversation.

The ridicule that had followed her all her life was not buried with her. At Curry's Bar that evening, a man greeted a friend with, "I heard you were a pallbearer out at Calvary Cemetery today," which brought laughter from the customers. And the man so greeted used the same line on the next to arrive.

A local man rushed to print sympathy cards and mailed them in envelopes edged in black to the homes of his friends, terribly upsetting a number of wives, who demanded explanations.

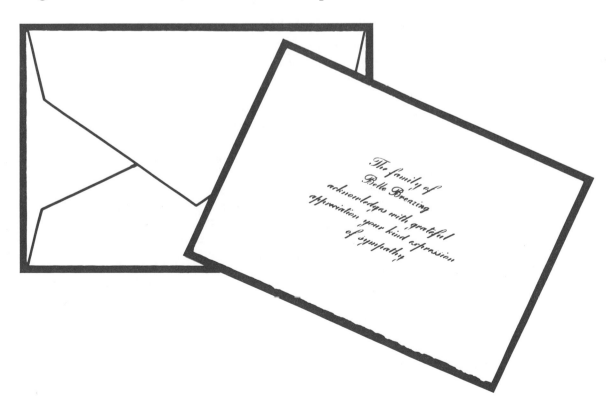

The family of
Belle Breazing
acknowledges with grateful
appreciation your kind expression
of sympathy

There were many who felt a deep loss at Belle's passing. Some had benefited from her generosity and fed their children in hard times because Belle had heard of their plight and opened her heart and her pocketbook.

Others felt the weight of their years as they read of her death and recalled the gentle kindness she had displayed when a physical need had confused them and there had been no one else who would understand.

Tandy Ellis wrote his friend in Lexington:

> Perhaps, somewhere, there is set aside a sequestered Island for the so-called lost souls, but these [women] of this oldest profession of the world might be the objects of a Merciful Creator. . . . I hope the soul of old Belle may land on the Island of peace and greet her old friends again.

The morning *Herald*, which had not yet informed its readers with even the small notice carried in the *Leader*, decided here was a story; and it went to work on it.

The Louisville Courier-Journal, in its trade paper, *Highlights and Shadows*, published an account of the manner in which the Lexington newspapers reported Belle's death.

> . . . A reporter was put to work on it, but his first draft was rejected because it was too vivid.
>
> Then J. R. "Babe" Kimbrough, acting city editor and veteran Herald legman, turned his attention to it. With Photographer Tom Stone, Kimbrough visited the Breazing home, interviewed a maid who had tended Miss Breazing for many years, and wrote his piece. Makeup editor put Kimbrough's story on page one, column one, along with a three-column cut of "Ghost House on North Eastern Ave."
>
> When the story reached the streets Tuesday morning, newsboys had no trouble in dispensing with their allotments. The circulation department sold 500 copies over the desk and newsstands and newspaper-selling stores put in a heavy demand for more copies. The entire edition of 19,000 copies was wiped out by 10 a.m. One cigar store held onto its last copy as customer-bait. Papers since then have been sold privately by citizens for 50 cents and $1.
>
> Circulation Manager Tom Adams said it was the first time in his recollection that a weekday Herald edition was sold out completely.
>
> Public reaction, at first, was indignant, most of the phoned complaints coming from women. . . .

It is hard to believe that in 1940 the subjects of Belle and the hill were still not considered fit conversation in mixed company.

—Herald Photo

A GHOST HOUSE ON NORTH EASTERN AVENUE—This house, once the scene of gaiety and revel, was silent last night—silent and lonely. For its aged owner was gone from the spacious old residence on North Eastern avenue where she had lived, almost alone, since changing customs deprived her of her occupation. Belle Breazing, one of the most widely known women in Lexington's history, had passed through its portals for the last time. (Other pictures on page 2).

End Comes To Belle Breazing

Dies At Ornate Old Home In Lexington

Death has closed another chapter of Lexington's history—a chapter which historians hesitated to write, but unwritten, had been elaborated until it had drifted well nigh into the field of legend.

Belle Breazing is dead.

This colorful character of the Gay Nineties and early Nineteen Hundreds succumbed early Sunday morning at her spacious brick residence on the southwest corner of North Eastern avenue and Wilson street.

She was buried yesterday afternoon in Calvary cemetery following brief committal services at the grave.

Once the operator of one of the largest and most lavish establishments south of the Mason-Dixon line, she had in recent years lived in seclusion in the dimly lit, decaying ruins of her once heavily gilded-and-mirrored "mansion for men." Her only companion was a Negro maid.

Had Passed 80th Birthday

Belle Breazing, who was past her eightieth birthday when death came, was reputed to have made and spent several fortunes. Yet Lexington's prototype of the Belle Watling of "Gone With the Wind" was noted for her sharp but fair methods of business dealing.

Charity, acquaintances said, took much of her earnings. But they expressed the belief that she had managed to retain at least a small portion of her wealth until the end.

The small yard surrounding the big red brick residence facing on North Eastern avenue had grown up in weeds. The ornamental iron fence had fallen to the ground.

Yet inside the building, amid fallen plaster and rotting woodwork, there remained last night much of the massive furniture which once had equipped the gay establishment.

Piano Stands Like Sentinel

The ballroom, with its red walls and mirrored ceiling, was still there. But all that remained of the room's furnishings was a huge mechanical piano standing like a mummified sentinel in one corner of the hall—its keys yellowed by the years and its handsomely carved cabinet lined with dust and cobwebs accumulated through decades of silence.

Almost intact was the private parlor which, according to legend, had been the scene of entertainment of many influential men.

In this room, decorated with a huge mirror which covered one wall, were still to be found the much-talked-about "horn chairs," fashioned from the horns of Texas steers, and upholstered in flaming red plush.

And the entrance hall with its richly carved stairway leading to the upper-floor apartments still held much of the glamor of the nights of long ago.

Wine Room Is Bare

At the rear of the first floor was the wine room which once had sheltered rare vintages. The old racks were still there, but they were empty. The doors of the huge cupboards stood ajar, their barren shelves covered with soot.

"Miss Belle had just let things go since she had been sick," the maid explained. "I haven't been in some of these rooms in years."

Monument To Gilded Era

The house, its furnishings and its dank atmosphere were a silent monument to the gilded era it represented. There was a strange sense of forlornness about it all—like a temple builded upon the sands that had been crumpled by the tide of moral righteousness.

Before establishing herself in the North Eastern avenue house, Belle Breazing was said to have conducted a similar establishment on North Upper street between Third and Fourth streets. Officials of the old Kentucky University, it was recalled, took steps to acquire the property and she was compelled to move.

Business flourished at the new location, it was said, until Camp Stanley was established here shortly before the United States entered the World War. Then a campaign was waged to close down such houses and she was forced to curtail operations.

In her girlhood, when she was described by acquaintances as "very good-looking," she had lived on West Main street near the Jefferson street viaduct.

She had been in poor health for several years. This, coupled with the infirmities of age, was given as the cause of death.

Surviving her is one daughter Daisy Kenney, of Dearborn, Mich.

—Herald Photos

PICTURES REVEAL FURNISHINGS OF BREAZING RESIDENCE—
Much of the massive furniture which once filled the big brick residence
of Belle Breazing at North Eastern avenue and Wilson street remains
among the decaying ruins of the establishment. The photograph at the
upper left shows the "horn chairs," fashioned from the horns of Texas
steers, which adorned the private parlor. At the lower left is a corner
view of the same room with its mirrored walls. In the photograph at
the upper right is shown a huge book-filled secretary, while at the
lower right is the mechanical piano in the ballroom of the house.

Nolan Carter, a well-liked young attorney (who later served as Master Commissioner for Fayette County and still later as judge in the circuit court), was appointed administrator of the estate and agreed with McFarland that, with all the publicity, the house should be cleared as quickly as possible.

Nine days after Belle was buried, the following ad appeared in the afternoon *Leader*.

Auctions

PUBLIC AUCTION

TO SETTLE THE ESTATE OF BELLE BREAZING
THURSDAY, AUGUST 22nd, 1940, AT TEN O'CLOCK A. M. PROMPT
CORNER OF NORTH EASTERN AVENUE AND WILSON STREET, LEXINGTON, KY.

Entire contents of building including large mirrors; famous horn suite furniture; cut-glass; silver; china; bric a brac of all kinds and other furniture.

Also, fifty-one pieces of jewelry consisting of a diamond necklace; diamond solitaire rings; diamond dinner rings; rings made of other precious stones; and other jewelry of gold and stones of many kinds.

NOLAN CARTER, Administrator of the Estate of Belle Breazing

SAM DOWNING, Auctioneer

Sam Downing turned off Main Street onto North Eastern early on the morning of the sale. He accelerated to climb the hill and rattled the old wooden bridge over the C. & O. tracks as he rolled into the red light district. He smiled to think that today he was going to do business "up on the hill." He remembered a time when he wouldn't have been caught dead up here. In fact, as a boy, if he had been seen "on the hill," he would have wished he were dead.

Sam was from a country background, a family of strong, attractive people who didn't hold with the seedy side of life these houses represented. But there were enough of the other kind of people to make the area hum through the Gay Nineties and well into the twentieth century.

Each house had a story, and Sam had heard most of them around the courthouse, where he held different positions in the county clerk's office in addition to being one of the most trusted and well-liked auctioneers of the time.

He turned his car into Wilson Street, backed out, and pulled down by the bridge. Sam was methodical; and his car was headed in the direction of home, waiting for his tired bones after what promised to be a "hard" sale. The auction itself had been set up by Nolan Carter, who had employed his wife and several other people to clean out the house and separate the wheat from the chaff. Sam climbed the steps, speaking to old customers and friends, and went in to see what was to be sold. He had heard that friends of McFarland and Carter had been allowed to come in the house and had bought quite a bit at "private sales" the day and evening before.

Nothing had been left in its original place. Tables held china, silver, and glassware. Stemware had been committed to boxes in an effort to match up sets. From silver candelabra to chipped potties, there seemed to be at least one of everything.

Fine cut glass; brass that once shone like new money, but now took on the look of unused pewter; bisque figurines; Imari vases, one five feet tall.

Belle's rosary had been dumped in a box with cheap jewelry left by girls leaving in haste, dreaming of better things.

Beautiful mahogany that once had known no rest between daily polishings now held the dust and grime of decades.

Parlor table and banquet lights, ironically now referred to as "Gone With the Wind" lamps, were brought to the downstairs front room, ready to be held up for the crowd to see.

Coin and sterling silver pitchers, vases, flatware, and service sets.

"Bellemobilia" — Belle's scrapbook, her little red journal, floor plan of the second floor of the Megowan Street house, handleless silver cups engraved "BB," the spoon given Belle on her thirty-second birthday by Billy Mabon. Other items are from the trash heap, collected in 1940 by Joe Jordan and Skeets Meadors. They include bills, cancelled checks, torn photographs, and a group of tintypes that, unfortunately, have no identification.

Dresser sets and engraved items, some reading "To Miss Belle from Pearl"; others, to "Kitten" — gifts from Billy Mabon with the pet name he always used for Belle. Several tea services on large trays. They had been a popular and expensive gift around the turn of the century.

There was the old horn furniture, sent to Belle by a Texas admirer. Leather-bound volumes of the classics in a tall walnut secretary.

Marble and onyx stands that once held figurines and statues that had appealed to Belle on sight when her pocketbook overflowed.

Things beyond redemption. Old mattresses. Bed springs, though pleasure bent, that had not squeaked in years. Rugs, faded and moth-eaten from years of neglect.

Fine gold leaf pier mirrors, so dirty they barely reflected. But once they had seen things not intended to be watched.

Daisy May's little rocking chair brought inquiries from the curious, but little interest from buyers.

Some of the items arranged for the auction sale of 1940.

Etagere photographed in 1940 just after Belle's death.

The empty wine room. Photographed in 1940.

Two handleless cups engraved "BB" and sterling spoon engraved in the bowl, "Kitten" (Billy Mabon's pet name for Belle). The spoon was a gift for her thirty-second birthday on June 16, 1892.

The following pictures were collected by Jordan and Meadors from the trash pile at the rear of 153 North Eastern Avenue just prior to the sale in 1940. The photographs of those girls whose names are known have been so identified.

Left — Studio photograph. The bottom had been torn off, possibly to destroy a name.
Right — Studio photograph of Lottie Brown.

Top left: Studio photograph of Georgie Lee, who also appears to Belle's left in the picture of 194 North Upper Street. Top right: Unidentified. Bottom left: Possibly one of Belle's maids, as she had only white "girls." Bottom right: Studio photograph by Mullen of Fannie Davis (Fannie Parshall), a friend of Belle's from her days at Jennie Hill's. Her obituary appears elsewhere in the text.

Top left: Unidentified. Top right: An attractive but unidentified young woman. Bottom left: This picture had been hand-colored and is considerably older than other photographs shown here. It possibly was someone from Belle's early years, perhaps her mother. Bottom right: Unidentified.

These and the following tintypes were bent when found after having been discarded. All are unidentified.

The "family entrance" as it appeared in 1940.

The main staircase photographed during preparations for the 1940 sale.

The night before the August 22, 1940, sale.

It was a couple of hours before sale time; but already people stood at the door, seeking entry to the largest by far of all the houses that had been the brothels of the Gay Nineties and Roaring Twenties. Some of the houses on North Eastern (still called Megowan by the old-timers), Wilson, and Curley were still operating, but with a far lower class of customer than in the old days. Many houses were now occupied by Negro families, who were slowly taking back what had once been a "colored section" free of bawdy houses. They were now appearing on their porches to watch the day's excitement. Belle had been buried only ten days, and there had been a flurry of activity for the past week in preparation for the sale.

Sam knew immediately that this would not be disposed of in a day; and he thought it advisable to sell the best things, hoping that some of the noisy crowd would dissipate and make it easier for his voice to be heard as he described each piece being held up and asked for an opening bid.

The sale was to start at ten o'clock; and by nine, the street was already full of people clamoring to get into the house. Police were called to rope off North Eastern to all traffic to prevent a passing motorist from running over a potential buyer. Finding the crowd too large to handle, Carter elected to keep everyone outside. But there are always old acquaintances who consider themselves privileged and insist they have only a few minutes to stay. (They are usually found to be the last to leave at the end of the day.) When Sam started, the crowd stretched all the way across North Eastern Avenue, into Wilson Street, and down North Eastern to positions where it would be almost impossible to identify the item being sold. Old customers of the house bumped elbows with the curious.

A Negro man on a porch across the street said, "Lord God, look at them white ladies goin' in that whorehouse."

First day of the sale, 1940. The gentleman in the center of the porch with his hand raised is auctioneer Sam Downing.

Coca-Cola sales were brisk in the heat from a cloudless sky, and soon stands were opened on the porches across from Belle's house. Buy 'em for a nickel, sell 'em for a dime. Women who had stood for hours and could stand no longer continued to stand, each item proving more interesting than the last and stirring great expectations as to what might come out next. Buyers who spent as much as $5.00 were allowed to enter the house for a look around.

Clara Sayre, Blanche Patterson, and other girls who had "boarded" at Belle's did not go to the sale. Perhaps they could not stand to see their alma mater dismantled in this way.

Clara stayed on the porch or in the yard of her little house on Curley Avenue and watched as people walked to their cars with armloads of "Miss Belle's treasures."

Ladies recognized by friends gave and received limp excuses as to why they were there. People yelled that their bids were not being seen; and sharp-elbowed dealers worked their way to the front of the crowd, ignoring requests that they stay off the steps and give the auctioneer room.

The jewelry sold the first day. It had been appraised by Victor Bogaert and was the highlight of the sale. Many fine items were engraved with Belle's name and the name of the presenter. Gentlemen who had been rash enough in their younger days to have their names etched on jewelry or silver were there to redeem the items regardless of price.

A man who purchased a diamond ring received jeers from his friends. "Hey, Charlie, how much did it cost you the first time you bought it?"

A young man from Nicholasville asked his aunt why a well-known Jessamine County landowner was bidding so vigorously on a fine gold pendant when he was so far back in the crowd he surely couldn't see it. "Don't worry," his aunt replied. "He's seen that necklace a hundred times."

All through the day, the relentless sun beat down on Sam as his chant, unaided by a speaker system, went out over the noisy crowd. Someone had placed a bisque figure of a fishing boy — intended for a fish bowl — on the side of a chamberpot. As it was held up, someone yelled, "Hey, Sam, what's that?" And Sam replied, "That's a curiosity, that's what it is. What am I bid?"

By midafternoon, when Sam had had all he could take, he told the crowd the sale was over for the day and to "Come back tomorrow." As he turned to go inside and see how much was left, the cries of "I've waited all day for one piece. Can't you sell it before you quit?" began. Sam had heard that line a thousand times, and he knew it was a ruse to get something cheap now that most of the people were hurrying to their cars.

Two Diamond Rings Bring Good Prices

A large crowd yesterday attended the auction sale of personal property belonging to the late Belle Breazing, conducted at the residence on the southwest corner of North Eastern avenue and Wilson street. Bidding was reported spirited. The sale will be resumed at 10 o'clock this morning. Among the higher-priced articles sold yesterday were two diamond rings which brought $600 and $550, respectively and a diamond necklace which sold for $450. A set of four chairs, fashioned from the horns of Texas steers, brought $50.

One night, as Belle showed her girls a diamond ring she had been given, a girl seemed ready to cry as she complained that she never got gifts from any of her regulars.

Belle put her arm around the girl and said, "Honey, those young boys promise themselves they'll never come back here again. And on Saturday night, by the time they can't fight the urge any longer, the stores are closed."

One particular item from Belle's sale was destined for an interesting role in the lives of its new owners. A gentleman and his wife purchased a large oil parlor lamp; its red shade and matching font were of satin glass. It certainly was a "red light" and exemplified the Victorian era in every respect.

The lamp was kept in a prominent place in the couple's home and was undeniably the conversation piece of the living room. Some years later, after the wife had died, the gentleman, in his loneliness, took a second wife. But this marriage proved to be far different from the harmonious union he had earlier enjoyed for so many years. For one thing, the new wife had little regard for the big red lamp and dusted it in a careless manner that terribly upset its owner.

As unpleasantness between the two increased, the man took to drink. On frequent occasions, he would, in the heat of an argument, try to rearrange his second wife's face and loosen a few of her teeth to make a point. The new wife, knowing of his love for Belle's relic, would run to the parlor and grab up the lamp. The husband, fearful of damaging this treasure, would stop in his tracks. As the woman walked about the house carrying the lamp, the man would first beg her to put it down and then threaten her life if she didn't.

Finally, when he passed out from drink and exhaustion, the crafty woman would go into another room and sleep the night away with the lamp still clutched in her arms. For the first wife, it had been a treasure; for the second, it was salvation.

The second day of the sale attracted as many people as the first, if not more. As Belle's beautiful dresses, some of them a half century old, were carried out and piled on the porch rail, they cascaded to the floor and to the ground below like a flowing rainbow. Women who bought armloads of dresses and capes said, embarrassedly, they would keep them to wear to tacky parties. Hats fashioned in Paris were worn down the street as the women left, followed by hoots of laughter from their friends.

By the end of the day, it seemed quite fashionable to be "up on the hill"; and in years to come, women would brag, "I went to that sale!"

The furniture was sold the third day, as Sam went from room to room, leaving the responsibility of carrying the massive pieces down the stairs to the buyers. Clara Sayre, who was told the furniture was being sold, hurried to the house, climbed the steps she had ascended so often in years past, and bought Miss Belle's bedroom suite. She paid $1,600.00 of the money Clem Beachey had left her for the furniture, but she would have paid twice that before she would have seen it go into strangers' hands.

By the end of the day, everything was sold and had been carted off. Furniture was finally loaded, and the rooms held only hollow echoes. That night, the house was locked; it stood quiet and lonely, a decaying relic of a bygone day, looming above the little sister houses that had also seen much better days. The following night the vandalism started; and by day and by night, the plumbing fixtures were stolen to be sold for whatever they would bring, windows were broken out by rock-throwing boys, the iron gates were taken from their hinges. Drunks slept on the parquet floors, while mice scurried about wondering what had happened to the grease drippings and crumbs they had always found in the kitchen.

By the time the house was sold a few months later, it took a discerning eye to imagine what it once had been. Like its mistress, it deserved better treatment.

Having been notified of Belle's death, the Probate Court for Wayne County, Michigan, appointed Floyd Frye guardian for Daisy May Kenney. He posted bond on October 23, 1940. With his application for appointment were filed two evaluations of Daisy's mental condition. One certified that, on examination,

> Her memory is very defective. When asked her age she says she is fourteen and that her mother is twelve. She cannot tell the year, month or date.
> Claims she will be married and every few days selects a different man as the groom elect.

The second evaluation states,

> She is full of notions and strange ideas. She is 40 years old. Says she is nineteen and her mother is sixteen. She has no connected ideas. She needs care in an institution.

The individual making the evaluation was evidently not informed that Daisy's true age was sixty-five.

Dr. Russell T. Costello, Chief of Staff at St. Joseph's Retreat, testified that Daisy May had been under his care and supervision for several years and, further:

> Daisy Kenney is feeble-minded and hopelessly incurable but . . . her

physical condition is excellent and . . . her life expectancy is much above the average.

Depositions were given by several Lexingtonians. James E. McFarland of the First National Bank and Trust Company stated the only information he had concerning her relatives was that,

> Daisy Kenney had two cousins who lived somewhere in the West. They were the sons of a deceased sister of Daisy Kenney's mother. Their name was Norton. I do not know their ages.

He estimated Belle's estate, real and personal, at $12,000.00.

Dr. C. A. Nevitt testified concerning Daisy May's relatives:

> My impression is from hearsay that she has two first cousins, but they have not been heard from in nine or ten years. We do not know whether they are living or dead. These two cousins are the sons of a deceased sister of Daisy Kenney's mother. My information is that their names are Carl Norton, who used to live on Vine Street, in Cincinnati, Ohio, and worked in a restaurant, and James Barry Norton, who lived in Vancouver, British Columbia, and was an actor. James had a wife and two children.

Dr. Nevitt, like McFarland, estimated the estate to be $12,000.00.

The Michigan court ruled that it had been proven, to its satisfaction, that Daisy May Kenney was an incompetent person. It authorized Floyd Frye to act as guardian and to enter into a "life support" contract with St. Joseph's Retreat and instructed him to turn over to St. Joseph's Retreat all the funds placed in his hands from the estate of Daisy May's mother. St. Joseph's Retreat agreed to furnish Daisy with

> . . . board, room, medical attention, clothing and other necessaries for the rest of her life, equal in quality to that furnished to the private patients and upon her death provide all of said patient's funeral expenses

in exchange for the monies in Frye's hands.

It was stated that Daisy May's life expectancy was 16.05 years, this in view of the fact that she was in good health and, being institutionalized, was not subject to the same likelihood of accidental death as a person living in the normal flow of life would be.

The net receipts from real and personal property, including the bank stock, totaled $8,318.54 after expenses; this amount was turned over to St. Joseph's Retreat.

In March of 1941, depositions were taken in connection with the sale of the real estate which had passed by Affidavit of Descent from the Estate of Belle Brezing to Floyd Frye as Guardian (Committee) for Daisy May Kenney.

In the testimony of A. S. Denny, a real estate agent, regarding this transfer, he described the North Eastern Avenue house as a three-story brick with metal roof, with twenty-five or thirty rooms and basement, all in very bad repair. He said the plumbing was old and out-of-date. Many fixtures had been removed, windows broken, etc. He estimated it would take four or five thousand dollars to put the house in livable condition. The missing fixtures and broken windows were undoubtedly a result of vandalism which occurred after the auction sale when the house stood unoccupied and unprotected.

Denny further testified that the property was built like a rooming house or hotel, with rows of rooms with numbers on the doors. He estimated the value of the house at the time at $3,000.00. On cross-examination, Denny stated that there was no other house in town like it and that he understood it to be a "house of bad repute." He added that the highest offer he had received for the house was $500.00 for the salvage of the brick.

C. E. Norman, another real estate agent, described the property in his testimony as a three-story brick building, with a hall running through the center, and in very bad repair. He stated that the house had been added to once. He also testified that there was no heating plant in the building, the paper was torn off, window cords were broken or gone, plumbing fixtures had been destroyed or taken away, heating plant was all out of repair, and the floors were in very bad condition.

Norman estimated that it would take $2,700.00 to put the house in repair. He also stated he had a party willing to pay $2,500.00 for the house, but that this party had not looked it over yet.

Both Denny and Norman described the house at 151 Dewees Street as a one-story frame house in very bad condition. When advised that the estate had received an offer of $1,300.00 for the property, the two men agreed it would be in the best interest of Daisy Kenney to accept the offer.

Dr. C. A. Nevitt, who also gave a deposition in this matter, testified that Belle had been a patient of his for about twenty-five years, was a widow at the time of her death, and had formerly been the wife of J. B. Kenney, "who died many years ago." Nevitt said Belle had one child, a girl named Daisy Kenney, who was a resident of an institution in Dearborn, Michigan, known as St. Joseph Retreat. He thought her age to be about sixty-four years. In answer to a question about Daisy's mental condition, the doctor replied that it was his understanding that she was an idiot.

The house on North Eastern Avenue, after suffering the ravages of time and the vandalism and theft of fixtures while it sat vacant for eight months, was finally sold to George Hoskins for $3,117.00 on April 21, 1941. Hoskins immediately transferred the property to his daughter and son-in-law, Mr. and Mrs. E. B. Sparks.

The Dewees Street property was sold to J. Rice Porter, also on April 21, 1941, for $1,300.00.

The net amount received from the sale of the two properties was paid over to St. Joseph's Retreat.

Nolan Carter made his final settlement as administrator of Belle's estate in November of 1944. The settlement indicated that, at the time of her death, Belle had in her checking account the amount of $124.76; that the auction sale of personal property had yielded $5,756.52; and that she owned thirty-six shares of stock of the First National Bank and Trust Company, Lexington, Kentucky, valued at $3,600.00.

Before turning the money over to Frye, Carter had paid all outstanding bills against the estate, including the auctioneer's fee of ten percent of the sale proceeds and all the expenses for setting up the sale (the advertising and the help hired in connection with the sale). Funeral expenses amounted to $350.00. He had also paid a claim from St. Joseph's Retreat in the amount of $1,567.50. This last item is very strange. It would indicate McFarland was far in arrears on the payments. It appears from the amount claimed that St. Joseph's, upon finding Belle had not been short of funds as the institution had been led to believe in 1913, had collected the difference between the reduced figure agreed on at that time and the regular fee.

The personal property in Belle's estate was sold in 1940 and the real estate in 1941. On today's market, the personal property would bring ten times as much; the real estate, considerably more, even though the area was then, and is now, depressed.

On August 3, 1948, Daisy May was sent from St. Joseph's Retreat in Dearborn to St. Mary's Hospital in Detroit. On August 5th, while still in the hospital, she suffered a broken hip and was operated on that same day (presumably to set the hip). She died on August 15th at St. Mary's.

St. Mary's Hospital later closed, and its records were transferred to the Detroit Memorial Hospital, which declines to give any information as to why Daisy May was hospitalized, how she broke her hip, or if she also suffered a broken neck, which seems to be indicated on the death certificate. The certificate states the immediate cause of death as "Pulmonary embolism." "Other contributory causes of importance" listed are fractured left femoral, neck. The legal department of the Michigan State Mental Health Department refused to intervene, saying the records are not subject to review because the subject was a mental patient.

Howe-Peterson Funeral Home handled the burial on August 19th at St. Hedwig Cemetery in Dearborn Heights. An order of Franciscan monks oversees the cemetery. A young man consulted his records and led the way to Section One, Lot One, where indigents are buried without any markers to indicate the graves. The monk explained that bodies are buried as they are received; by counting from the first grave, it is possible to locate a particular one. And he indicated the spot where Daisy May is buried.

CHAPTER 9

The Last Red Light Goes Out

The hill continued to be the center of the red light district although there were few "houses"; these no longer attempted to be the entertainment centers that had flourished before World War I. Negro families had moved back into most of the houses, and the few establishments that still existed were on Wilson Street and Curley Avenue. Old Megowan Street, which had once had fifteen houses and over seventy-five girls, now — as North Eastern Avenue — had one house with a single girl. There were only ten houses in operation in Lexington in 1940, and two of these were outside the old district: one on North Broadway and one on West Fifth Street. There was a "call" house on Kenton Street, back of Transylvania College, where the madam could arrange for a woman to be there for a rendezvous. The old desire to find a young girl who was not really a prostitute continued, and rumor said the girls on Kenton were Transylvania students who needed money to stay in school. This, of course, was not the case. For the most part, they were working girls in town who supplemented their incomes in this manner. There were a few wives who could be called for "nooners" or afternoon appointments when they would not be missed at home.

Several of the houses in the old district had only one girl; two had five; but as in the old days, the girls came and went. All were dollar houses; but when they got a new girl, the madam would try for $2.00 for her "special attraction."

Clara Sayre lived quietly in her little house; but Blanche Patterson, who had fallen on hard times, had one girl, a most unfortunate creature known as "One Arm Lula," who sat on the porch swing, positioned so that it was not obvious that her right arm was missing.

One house on Curley Avenue (East Short Street Extended) still had a dance room, but it was a far cry from Belle's fancy ballroom. The floor had a worn Congoleum rug; there were two old, overstuffed couches, and a nickel juke box. After eleven o'clock, when most of the night's business was over, the house and its three girls could be "bought out" for $10.00 or $20.00. Boys, fresh from dates with "nice girls," could dance and take any one of the girls, or all three in turn, to a room. No alcohol was sold, but a girl would go to the corner and bring back beer if a client paid for it.

When asked, the girls usually said they were from West Virginia; as in the old days, they said they were taken advantage of in a dentist's chair, while under the influence of gas. This had led to their downfall. It made a good story and helped them avoid the heartache of remembering what had really led them into the profession.

On summer evenings, the girls would lounge about on a front porch and beckon to slow-moving cars that cruised by to look over the "merchandise." On colder days, they sat by a front window, tapping on the glass with a key or coin as the cars paraded by. Boys would sometimes take their dates for a cruise on the hill. The girls, sitting low in the seat so they couldn't be seen, were fascinated by the calls their boyfriends would get from the porches.

If a prostitute was young and attractive, she would sit by a lamp so that she could more easily be seen from the street. The older and less attractive women placed the light slightly behind them and remained partly in shadow, hoping the element of mystery would help.

Some of the little shotgun houses like Blanche Patterson's had only one girl. She would use the back bedroom, making it necessary for the men to pass through the front room, where the madam sat collecting money. On leaving, they would see the next customer awaiting his turn.

When a customer entered one of the larger houses (still small by the old standards) on Curley Avenue, all the girls available would be called into the parlor so that the man could make his choice. The girls stood mutely, like cattle, as they awaited selection or rejection. If a girl was chosen, she took the man to her room, made a whore's quick inspection, and looking into the customer's eyes, asked, "You ain't got nothin', have you, honey?" Then, as she quickly disrobed, she would say, "Last night a fellow tipped me 50¢, and last week a real nice guy gave me $5.00." It was worth a try. She was getting only half of the dollar that had been paid the madam, and she had board to pay. For a dollar, the man didn't get much other conversation except to be told to "hurry up."

Mrs. Egbert still hobbled about on her cane, usually in the shadow of the old warehouse that had at one time been the hospital. She knew she would not be backed up if she tried to trouble the girls, except where juveniles were concerned. It always scared a madam when she saw young boys coming up the walk; she would hurry them in and look up and down the street to see if the policewoman was in sight.

Although the hill no longer held the interest it once had for wealthy gentlemen, it continued to have a certain attraction for young people, who viewed the unfortunate girls with the same fascination they would animals in a zoo.

As a part of fraternity initiations, college boys were sometimes required to make a drawing of the floor plan of one of the "houses." The madams, for the most part, seemed to cooperate as much as possible with the strange requests they received from embarrassed young men. Blanche Patterson would allow a boy to measure the rooms on the first floor, but he was barred from climbing the stairs without the proper payment.

When fountain service to cars was first introduced in town, pranksters stole the freestanding "Curb Service" signs and placed them in front of the houses on the hill. The next day, the signs were retrieved by their rightful owners, only to be carried back to the hill on the next prom night or on Halloween.

December 7, 1941, "a day that will live in infamy," brought war less than twenty-five years after "the war to end all wars." The shadows fell once more over the land; this time, the hill was destined for final darkness.

Draftees and volunteers were shipped into town for training at Transylvania and the University of Kentucky. All the doors were stripped from the rooms at the Phoenix Hotel, and it became an Army barracks. Boys, many of whom had never left the farm before, discovered the hill. Once again, the Army pronounced Lexington a wicked city. In 1917, the New York papers had reported Lexington as the third most evil city in America; this time, it was not rated quite so high, but there was still great concern.

The houses were once again closed; the girls, for the most part, moved out of town to cheap hotels near Army bases or became streetwalkers in some war-economy boom town. A few hung out in local bars; but every time a soldier failed a monthly V. D. exam, the local police were notified, and the ladies of the evening were rounded up and jailed or headed out of town.

Belle's old house had been repaired and was rented to Flora Hudson, a pixie of a black lady with a kindly smile, who opened it as the Hudson Hotel. Colored soldiers traveling through Lexington found there were no overnight accommodations, and Flora entered into a contract with the Army to house them. Sometimes there were thirty-five or forty boys staying overnight. The Army paid the vouchers by the month.

The City Manager, determined to comply with the Army's wishes, went to Clara Sayre's house (everyone knew she had not operated in years) and told her she most sell out and leave. She went into the house and returned with her savings account book. She had lived frugally and still had most of the money Clem Beachey had left her. With her eyes snapping, she showed the balance to the official and said, "You make me move, and I'll buy the house next door to you, no matter what the damned thing costs." She had no further trouble.

Clara, who had been estranged from her family since she left Cincinnati so many years earlier, made peace with her brother before she died a few years later in her little house. Once more in the good graces of her family, she was cared for in her last illness by her niece.

When Blanche Patterson's house was closed, she retired from the profession and lived on the second floor of a building on the southeast corner of Church Street and Broadway.

I interviewed a gentleman who said Blanche became "perty sorry" in her last days. She made a fortune on men and spent it on other men. It is said that Blanche gave Joe Keith the money to open his first bar on Limestone Street.

Later, old acquaintances took pity on her. She was given a job as chambermaid at a flophouse hotel on South Broadway. She died penniless. A local man, who remembered her in better times, paid for her funeral.

Negro families soon moved into the houses vacated by the madams. Once more, after over a half a century of intrusion, the hill belonged to the black residents.

Flora Hudson continued to rent Belle's old house until the mid-1960's, when the ever-evolving building regulations classified it below standard as a hotel. The owners then converted the building to thirteen apartments and gave it a new name: the Floral Apartments. The name was in recognition of Flora's long occupancy.

At 3:42 p.m. on December 12, 1973, the Lexington Fire Department responded to an alarm; the location was North Eastern and Wilson Street. When the first truck arrived, smoke was billowing from Belle's old house; and a woman was trapped on the third floor (nearly the same conditions firemen had found seventy-eight years before).

Firemen from eight units answered the 3:42 P.M. call on Wednesday, December 12, 1973. The American Red Cross served hot coffee and sandwiches to the firemen and police.

The news release tells the story.

NEWS RELEASE:

ARSON DIVISION, LEXINGTON METRO FIRE DEPARTMENT (MAJOR BOB WORKS) 12–17–73

The cause of the fire that occurred in an apartment house at 153 North Eastern Ave. at 3:42 P. M., Wednesday, December 12th, 1973, has been officially determined.

A 7 year old male juvenile admitted squirting lighter fluid over some furnishings in his apartment, and according to this statement, he squirted the lighter fluid on an open flame gas room heater in the bedroom. The heater ignited the fluid and a flash fire resulted, spreading to the contents of the apartment. The juvenile (boy) escaped the flames by jumping from a second story window of his apartment to the top of a car parked below. He suffered no injuries in the fire, nor in his jump from the window.

A 37 year old woman, identified as Carol Smith, was trapped in her 3rd floor apartment above the fire. She was rescued by Metro Firemen and transported to Good Samaritan Hospital by the Fire Dept. Emergency Medical Care Unit; however, she expired at 3:10 A. M., Friday morning, Dec. 14th, as a result of her burns and smoke inhalation.

The fire gutted several apartments and the roof and attic of the apartment house, resulting in several thousands dollars loss to both building and contents. The building is owned by Mr. E. B. Sparks of Lexington.

The unfortunate Carol Smith was survived by her mother, Mrs. Jane Krycier of Akron, Ohio; the body was sent to the Armstrong Funeral Home, Seville, Ohio.

The building seemed to be beyond economical repair; but E. B. Sparks, the owner, was approached by Joe Graves, Jr., and Bill Rice, local businessmen, who thought it had great possibilities as a restaurant. Sparks held up the demolition, but the restaurant plan never materialized. The building inspector's office wanted a decision on what was to be done with the structure as it represented a hazard after the fire. An auction was arranged to sell all the architectural features that could be removed, and an auction notice appeared in the newspapers and in handbills.

On the day of the auction, one of the first men to arrive said that he had heard one of Belle's old girls was coming to the sale. Shortly afterwards, a chauffeur-driven limousine pulled up in front of the house and two elderly ladies, very tastefully dressed, were helped from the car by the driver. Each carried a gold-headed cane, and each wore a black velvet throat ribbon such as those worn by dowagers at the turn of the century.

On entering the house, they went from room to room, looking at each wall, ceiling, floor, and doorway. As they started up the steps to the second floor, they were cautioned by the auctioneer to be careful because the upper floors were wet from the water used in fighting the fire and the rains that had fallen since the roof had burned. On the second floor, they went from room to room. Occasionally, one would point with her cane. The rooms were empty. There was nothing to point to unless to indicate where some piece of furniture had stood or where some event had occurred. After inspecting the entire second floor, they returned to the automobile and left.

Everything was sold that could be pried loose in the house. The mantels, the gold picture molding, the doors, the inside shutters, "the family entrance." Even scraps of wallpaper were sold; a small section with cherubs went to the mayor. A Tennessee man, reported to be an architect or designer, purchased one entire room. It was said that it was to be installed near Nashville as a den in the home of a famous country singer.

A few days later, a bulldozer leveled the house. The bricks were taken away to be sold later as souvenirs. Soon there was nothing to show where Belle's "palace of pleasure" had been. A landmark was gone, and the last remnant of the hill's gilded age was only a memory.

AUCTION

Of Memorabilia, From The Most Orderly Of Disorderly Houses

153 NORTHEASTERN — LEXINGTON, KY.

10:30 A.M. Saturday, March 23, 1974

In 1890, a secret admirer built, for Madam Belle Breezing, a "Sporting house" that was to become the most famous and elegant "house of ill repute" the decade would see. When Miss Belle died in 1940, Time Magazine reported her death, and described her establishment as "the most orderly of disorderly houses". Her guest list was virtually a "Who's Who of prominent personalities and the dandies of the turn of the century."

On the night of December 12th, the house that had later been operated as an apartment house and hotel, suffered the ravages of a devastating fire. The owners, finding th building beyond economical repair, are forced to raze the structure.

Little is left of the elegance that had paid host to the famous and infamous of a bygone era. Wallpaper in a cherub pattern hangs water soaked from the ceiling, in a room that once echoed to the call of "ladies to the parlor." The wood of a parquet floor, loosed by fire hoses, lie like children's blocks scattered in an empty hall. Mantel mirrors that once reflected candlelight, now look out on the decay of another life.

True, little is left, but who of you can dream a "back bar" from an old mantel, or a use for old gold molding in the parlor ceiling, a curio box or desk ornament from floor blocks; who will bid on the iron mantel from Miss Annie's room for a conversation piece in a den or recreation room; start the bidding on a stained glass window that illuminated the stairs where satin mustled skirts led the way to the second floor; who can use a gingerbread stairway that could tell a thousand tales? How about bricks for a fireplace or a garden wall? What can be made of old door facings or the inside shutters that separated "fallen flowers" from the prime Victorian world outside?

If you can't stand quietly, in the midst of clutter, and hear soft voices, the tinkle of Champagne glasses, or the wail of a down hearted frail floating back over the years, don't bother to come. It's a spooky old house; and we have nothing to sell but nostalgia.

TERMS: (As Belle Would Say) are Cash; and Inspection is at time of Sale. Removal of sale items is responsibility of the buyer.

E. I. (Buddy)
Thompson
200 N. Upper
Phone 252-6677

Thompson & Riley
Realtors
AUCTIONEERS

J. L. (Jim)
Riley
714 E. Main
252-3117

24 — AUCTIONS — 24

Epilogue

A comparison of the life of Belle Brezing and the fictional character of Belle Watling makes it obvious that John Marsh had told his wife tales of Brezing and that Margaret Mitchell drew on these to create Belle Watling.

Both met with rejection in their efforts to help a hospital. Both were noted for the fact that their girls were quieter than the other girls in the district. Both had a child said to be away at school. Both had fine carriages and a Negro coachman.

The houses of both women were paid for by wealthy benefactors and were much larger than the bawdy houses around them. The fine furniture, large mirrors, oil paintings, Negro orchestra, downstairs barroom, and other points of similarity are undeniable.

Although I found no reference to Brezing having the flaming red-dyed hair attributed to Belle Watling, one of her pictures indicates she had changed the color of her hair. Even though we cannot tell the color from the old black and white picture, we can see that it is considerably lighter than in other photographs. According to Anne Edwards, Margaret Mitchell was told by one of her husband's friends of Brezing's red hair.

No matter what her life had been, Belle Brezing is a part of Lexington's history and is firmly established as a Kentucky legend. She was the prototype for Belle Watling in a book second only to the Bible in the number of copies printed.

Picture frames made from the molding in her house are frequently more interesting than the pictures they encase.

Gavels made from timbers of the old structure are used as exceptional presentation pieces to dignitaries in ceremonies.

Fireplaces built of bricks from the old house are conversation pieces in fine homes, and other bricks have been used in walls to enclose gardens.

An entire room is the pride of a millionaire singer's home. The door from the "family entrance" is used as an office entrance.

Copies of Belle's picture hang in homes, taverns, and shopping centers.

Artists have painted Belle; some have painted her house. Prints of these paintings are to be found on the market today, as well as note paper with the old house as it appeared in its heyday.

Her dresses are prized possessions of theater groups and private collectors. On occasion, a lady has been known to wear one of Belle's capes to dances at the country club.

In homes from Philadelphia to California, women point with pride to mementoes from Belle's house. At auction, articles of furniture and bric-a-brac sell for a hundred times the amount they brought in 1940.

A recent history of Lexington, printed by the Lexington-Fayette County Historic Commission, would be incomplete were it not for the half-page picture of Belle and a capsule version of her life.

Newspapers hardly go a month without some mention of Belle. Three booklets have been written which, although containing some inaccuracies, relate vignettes of her life.

The Lexington Trots Breeders Association in 1983, almost a half century after her death, inaugurated an annual three-year-old filly race at the famous Red Mile, with a $15,000.00 purse, to be known as The Belle Breezing Pace. In conjunction with the first running of the race, a "Belle Breezing Look-alike" contest was held, with fifteen young ladies participating. The winner received a $500.00 prize.

The mention of her name still offends some and evokes snide remarks from others.

She is referred to as a common whore, a flashy prostitute, and a notorious madam. But she is also the little girl who, on her first day at school, stung by rejection, held back tears as, she said, "I'll say what I want and do what I want, and to hell with all of you!"

Notes

4   The Barrow Unit was organized by Dr. David Barrow of Lexington, Kentucky, and consisted of eight doctors, twenty-nine nurses, and seventy-five enlisted men. They were inducted as Base Hospital No. 40 and left Lexington in 1918. Many of its members were well-known Lexingtonians, who willingly performed menial tasks in an effort to relieve the suffering of American soldiers. Several reunions were held, and it was at one of these that Marsh allegedly referred to Belle Brezing.

6   Belle's name was engraved with one "e" — Brezing — on the silver nameplate from the front door of the house at 194 North Upper Street.

7   The often-told story that Belle was able to pay off a loan prematurely because a Baptist convention had been held in Lexington is an example of such a story told in other states about other prostitutes and madams.

12   Copyright 1940 Time Inc. All rights reserved. Reprinted by permission from *Time*.

13   Woodford County, Kentucky Order Book H, 1846–1857, page 450. Special Collections, Margaret I. King Library, University of Kentucky Libraries.

13   Woodford County, Kentucky, Vital Statistics. Box 29, Microfilm. Special Collections, Margaret I. King Library, University of Kentucky Libraries.

14   Jessamine County, Kentucky Order Book E, pages 44–45. Microfilm. Kentucky Historical Society Library.

15   Marriage Book 3, page 152, Fayette County Courthouse.

15   Linda Neville (1873–1961) lived until her death in the same house in which she was born at 722 West Main Street in Lexington, Kentucky. She dedicated her life to work with the blind. Miss Neville was interviewed by Joe Jordan.

20   Civil Orders Book 47, June 19, 1866, Fayette County Courthouse. The judge who granted the divorce was the Hon. William Cassius Goodloe, a nephew of the famed abolitionist Cassius Marcellus Clay. He had been in his uncle's service when the latter, appointed by Presi-

Page

dent Abraham Lincoln, served as minister to the court of the czar of Russia during the American Civil War. Goodloe was also the same man who, in 1889, fought Armstead Swope in a duel to the death in the lobby of the old Lexington Post Office. Both men died in that duel, Goodloe of bullet wounds from Swope's pistol and Swope from the stab wounds inflicted by a bowie knife Cassius Clay had given his nephew to be used against this enemy.

Depositions in the divorce trial were given before Judge James Mulligan, owner of Maxwell Place (now the home of the president of the University of Kentucky), who at one time was Consul to Samoa, friend of Robert Louis Stevenson, and author of the famous poem, "In Kentucky."

21 In pioneer days, when no preacher was available to perform the ceremony, a couple could signify their marriage in the presence of witnesses by jumping over a broomstick. This was considered sufficient to hold them until the next traveling preacher arrived to solemnize the union.

21 *Lexington Observer and Reporter*, November 10, 1869. *The Kentucky Gazette*, November 13, 1869. Lexington Cemetery records show burial in Section K, Lot 13.

21 Divorcees (grass widows) frequently referred to themselves simply as widows.

22 Marriage Book 5, page 62, Fayette County Courthouse. *The Kentucky Gazette*, October 28, 1871, page 3.

22 D. Mucci & Bro. purchased one blind bay horse and wagon from Lewis Jenkins, June 17, 1872. Mortgage Book 1, page 304, Fayette County Courthouse.

D. Mucci & Bro. purchased from John Hudson one bay horse and spring wagon painted drab color, December 22, 1873. Mortgage Book 2, page 184, Fayette County Courthouse.

22 Criminal Court Records, page 159, Commonwealth Causes, General Index, #1:
Commonwealth vs. E. Mucci, Box 5   1876
Commonwealth vs. Z. Mucci and
                         C. Mucci, Box 43   1876
Commonwealth vs. Emile Mucci, Box 59   1880
Fayette County Courthouse.

23 Zachariah lived in Georgetown, Kentucky, at one time. Records (incomplete) of the Georgetown Cemetery do not indicate any of the Mucci women being buried there.

23 It was only after Mrs. Josephine K. Henry and Mrs. Sarah G. Humphreys, both of Versailles, Kentucky, and Mrs. Mary K. Jones of Newport, Kentucky, working for the Kentucky Equal Rights Association, brought pressure to bear on the General Assembly that the age of consent was raised to sixteen in 1893.

26 Slaves came to Lexington during the Civil War in order to be under the protection of the Northern forces. The children undoubtedly admired their emancipators, which might explain the Union caps.

Page

28   Lexington Cemetery record: Willie Sutphin, Buried May 24, 1874, Lot 58, Grave 5½, #6163. *Lexington Daily Press*, May 21, 1874, page 4, column 1. *Lexington Daily Press*, May 23, 1874, page 4, column 5.

30   Marriage Book 5, pages 224–225, Fayette County Courthouse.

30   *Lexington Daily Press*, September 15, 1875, page 4, column 2.

31–32   *Lexington Daily Press*, September 24, 1875, page 4, columns 2 and 3.

33   *Lexington Daily Press*, September 25, 1875, page 4, column 2.

34   *Lexington Daily Press*, September 28, 1875, page 4, column 3.

35   *The Lexington Herald*, August 23, 1915, page 10, column 4.

35   Johnny Cook buried in Lexington Cemetery, Section N, Lot 7. The cemetery record for Johnny Cook reads "Koche." But the stone on the grave reads "John Andrew Cook."

James Kenney buried in Lexington Cemetery, Section C-1, Lot G, Grave 33.

D. Mucci buried in Calvary Cemetery, Section J.

Sarah McMeekin buried in Calvary Cemetery, Section O, Lot 6.

Belle Brezing buried in Calvary Cemetery, Section O, Lot 6.

35   Miss Neville recalled that Belle left town for a short time shortly after these events, but perhaps she merely stayed confined to the house. In any case, she was not seen in Lexington during her pregnancy.

Joe Jordan examined Belle's Bible in 1940 and noted that the child was listed as Daisy May Lewis. In that Jordan retyped these notes, as did Mrs. Meadors, it appears they would have caught this if it were a copying error. It could be possible, if the entry had been copied correctly, that Belle knew the true father of the child and that his name was Lewis.

36   Mrs. Margaret Egbert was interviewed by Burton Milward on March 28, 1940. She said she was a little older than Belle when they both attended Dudley School. "We kids couldn't understand why our families wouldn't let us have anything to do with her."

40   As a child, Belle went to Broadway Christian Church, but later joined the Catholic church since her mother had been a Catholic (Burton Milward interview with Mrs. Egbert).

41   Jennie Hill was not listed in the *Lexington City Directory* prior to the 1879–80 edition, the information for which was probably gleaned in 1878. This is further proof that Belle could not have gone to Jennie Hill's immediately following her mother's funeral in 1876, one of the common misconceptions about Belle.

Selby Lilliston (Georgetown, Kentucky) purchased the Mary Todd Lincoln property on May 25, 1870. Deed Book 47, page 603, Fayette County Courthouse.

41   J. Tandy Hughes came to Lexington in 1871 when he was four years old. Throughout his life, he was an interested observer of the personalities and events of Lexington and knew a great deal about the hill and its operation. It was said Pearl Hughes took her name from

Page

Tandy. Although past ninety when interviewed by Meadors, he recalled Hale's song word-for-word.

45 Mortgage Book 7, page 196, Fayette County Courthouse.

45 Mortgage Book 7, page 218, Fayette County Courthouse.

46 This was the first of many occasions when Belle would be in conflict with the forces of law and order. See separate listing.

47 This is the journal the late William H. Townsend acquired under circumstances described in his pamphlet, "The Most Orderly of Disorderly Houses." In the late 1930's, Townsend received a call from Belle's doctor, C. A. Nevitt, inquiring if Townsend was on the book committee of the University of Kentucky Library and saying he had an elderly patient who had a valuable book collection she would give to the University if it were interested.

Townsend took Dr. Thomas D. Clark, Samuel M. Wilson, and J. Winston Coleman, Jr., all historians and booklovers, and visited Miss Belle, the patient the doctor spoke of. Several books were selected; and when Townsend discovered the "little journal," fearing Belle would not want it in circulation, he placed it under his vest. Townsend's daughter, Mary Genevieve Murphy, and her husband, Joe Murphy, made it available in order that the information it contained could be included in this book.

48 Margaret Mitchell was asked several times why Belle Watling's house did not have a parrot as they were almost a standard fixture in the early houses.

There are two references that indicate Belle Brezing had a bird. In addition to the entry in the little journal, Tandy Hughes stated in his interview: "That sister of Billy Mabon's was married to Dick Morgan. She kept Belle's parrot." There is no information as to when or why she kept the bird, but she must have been an understanding soul. Most of the parrots were taught all the four-letter words and many phrases that surely would have curled the hair of a lady of Mrs. Morgan's standing. (Mrs. Morgan is further identified in a later reference.)

48 Tandy Ellis said the first woman he ever saw smoke a cigarette was at Belle's place.

49 There was no family in Lexington whose name could have been confused with Belle's.

51 *The Daily Lexington Transcript*, May 2, 1883, page 1, column 4.

51 Deed Book 68, page 189, Fayette County Courthouse.

53 *Lexington Daily Press*, March 12, 1882. Lexington Cemetery record: Fannie Parshall buried March 11, 1882, Section G-1, Lot 120, Grave 44.

53 Mrs. Egbert was a student at Hamilton College, which was located on North Broadway not far from 194 North Upper Street. She and several friends passed the new house and saw the party in full swing.

58 Most of the information regarding Charles C. Moore was taken from his book, *Behind the Bars*.

Page

59 *Lexington Observer and Reporter*, March 7, 1849.

59 The Megowans were a prominent family in Lexington. The elder Megowan was well-known as a supporter of his church and a pillar of the community.

61 Simon B. Buckner Papers, Governors' Papers, Kentucky Historical Society. On deposit in Department for Libraries and Archives, Commonwealth of Kentucky.

62 Charles Morris, *Makers of Philadelphia*. Jamersly, 1894, page 192.

62 Deed Book 88, page 323, Fayette County Courthouse.

64 William H. Townsend reported ("The Most Orderly of Disorderly Houses," page 6) that girls were also brought in from Memphis, Nashville, and St. Louis. It is impossible to confirm this on independent grounds.

64 William H. Townsend and others reported seeing a picture made on the occasion of the grand opening. If this picture still exists, its whereabouts are unknown to me. The photo was supposedly taken of the girls and the guests in the front yard of the house. Townsend stated he recognized a number of prominent citizens among the guests. He stated the picture gave a date in 1891. However, Belle's first liquor license confirms that the house was originally opened for business in 1890.

64 Electricity did not come to Lexington until 1882. By 1890, there were only seventy-five houses with electric service. Since power was available only during certain hours, even these houses still had to rely on gas for lighting. Belle's was probably one of the first houses to have the new chandeliers made expressly for gas and electricity. In other homes, earlier gas chandeliers were converted to accommodate electricity on alternate arms. Bettye Lee Mastin, "Now and Then," *The Lexington Herald*, August 3, 1982.

70 The spoon and the book are both in the author's collection.

72 Mabon did not get his apartment on Cheapside until after the date of Singerly's death contrary to other reports stating his apartment was on Cheapside during this period.

74 After a year of searching, in which it seemed it would be impossible to determine the whereabouts of Daisy May during this period of her life, her name was at last found by Linda Ashley in the 1910 census records for Detroit. This discovery eventually provided the solution to the question of where Daisy had lived between 1894 and the time of her death.

75 In 1902, the street numbers were changed. Belle's house, originally 59 Megowan Street, was renumbered to 153 Megowan Street. In the 1907–08 *City Directory*, the section listing persons gives Belle's address incorrectly as 163 Megowan Street; the section listing streets shows 153 Megowan Street.

76 Joe Jordan gave Burton Milward the picture of Belle's house before the third floor was added. Seemingly, neither Jordan nor Milward realized it was a two-story version of the house.

Page

79   R. P. Moloney, Sr., was the father of the late state senator R. P. Moloney.

80   Some typical books used to instruct children in sex and marriage are the following:
Marriage. Boston Monday Lecture Series. Joseph Cook.
Transmission of Life. Dr. George H. Napheys.
Physical Life of Gentlemen. Dr. George H. Napheys.
Physical Life of Women. Dr. George H. Napheys.
Drawn from Life. Sketches of Young Ladies, Young Gentlemen, and Young Couples. Charles Dickens.
Manhood and Marriage. Bernarr Macfadden.
The Virile Powers of Superb Manhood. Bernarr Macfadden.
The Woman Worth While. Susanna Cocroft.
Four Monster Temptations. W. F. Bischoff.

82   Belle's bedroom, and each of the girls', had a couch at the foot of the bed of the type usually referred to as fainting couches. These may have been used to keep from mussing up the bed so that it would not have to be remade each time.

89   Singerly's financial failures occurred at a time when the nation's economy was still suffering the effects of the Panic of 1893. His obituary notice in the *Philadelphia Record*, February 28, 1898, quotes from the notices which appeared in various publications on the occasion of his death, and several references are made to "the dark chapter which ended his career" and "dark clouds of sadness and misfortune" surrounding the collapse of his financial interests.

92   Dr. C. A. Nevitt, who is referred to a number of times in the Jordan/Meadors interviews and who gave depositions in legal matters concerning Belle's daughter, Daisy May Kenney, was Belle's long-time personal physician and was frequently used by girls on the hill.

93   Interview with Virgil Linkenfelter, August 15, 1982. As a young man, Mr. Linkenfelter worked at Meyers.

93   Mary McCarthy, another Lexington madam, frequently went to the trots with her girls. Mrs. A. R. Musser, a long-time Lexington resident with a keen memory and a great interest in local history, said in her interview that they were very loud and profane.

101   Mrs. Egbert said that Broaddus' father, knowing his son frequented Belle's house, had warned her that his son was irresponsible and sometimes became violent when under the influence of spirits (Burton Milward interview).

Testimony at the inquest into the death of Debbie Harvey, given by John H. Flood (attorney for Broaddus), stated the "defendant at that time was insane and not responsible for his conduct." He also said Broaddus had been subject to periodic fits of insanity, once had tried to kill his father, and had been a patient at Eastern Kentucky Lunatic Asylum. In addition, Broaddus' mother, father, and sister also had been subject to spells of insanity. *The Lexington Leader*, October 2, 1911.

Page

102 Commonwealth vs. Oliver Broaddus, Box 222, Commonwealth Causes, Criminal Court Records, Fayette County Courthouse (Broaddus indicted by grand jury). *The Lexington Herald*, July 9, 1911, page 3, columns 3 and 4. *The Lexington Herald*, July 12, 1911, page 1, column 4; page 4, column 1; page 10, column 3.

102 Lexington Cemetery record: Oliver D. Broaddus, age 30, Buried October 2, 1914, Section 13, Lot 47, #19227, Late residence: Arcadia, Florida.

102 Lexington Cemetery record: Debbie Harvey, age 23 [sic], Interred July 11, 1911, Section D-1, Lot A, Grave 29, #17951.

104 *The Lexington Leader*, July 11, 1911.

106 Mrs. Egbert said Belle had several peddlers who were procurers for her (Joe Jordan interview). She also said that a local character named Buz Ray procured girls for Belle in the mountains (Burton Milward interview).

108 1909 *Lexington City Directory* lists the residence of John J. Riley as 145 Dewees Street.

108 Mrs. Musser says Lilly Bowman, one of Belle's girls, married Mr. Ralph Greenbaum of Midway, who owned the distillery there.

109 Other prostitutes who had come from the hill and tried to lead respectable lives without the advantage of a husband with some standing in the community found little acceptance. I recall an example of this when I was a child. A woman attending a service in a Methodist church was asked to move from the seat she had selected because it had customarily been occupied by a lady now deceased and should not now be used by a woman of ill fame.

112 Belle would not let her girls go out without an escort (Mrs. Egbert interview with Burton Milward).

113 John Coyne, bartender, said the name of the man who reserved Belle's house for the race meet was Bonner. Chinn interview as reported by Meadors gives name as Baunta.

113 I was in Mollie Irvine's house long after she was dead; the house was still in the family, owned by her granddaughter. It was no longer a "house," but a "home." In the back hall on the wall was a picture of the old place when it was new. Mollie stood on the porch with her girls standing around in the yard. They were beautiful girls, tastefully dressed in the long dresses and bustles of the time. Mollie's granddaughter said I could copy the picture, but the house burned before I got around to it, and I suppose the picture burned with it.

115 The name of the Protestant Infirmary was changed in 1899 to Good Samaritan Hospital.

118 Billy Mabon's grave is next to the Hunt family circle.

120 *The Lexington Leader*, October 24, 1917.

122 *The Lexington Leader*, October 31, 1917.

Page

122   The Lexington papers devoted considerable attention to the vice conditions in Lexington with almost daily reports from October 17 through November 4, 1917. Information in this section has been gleaned from these articles.

126   19th Amendment (Woman Suffrage) ratified August 28, 1920.

127   *The Little Folks' Speaker or Songs and Rhymes for Jolly Times*, by Florence Underwood Colt. Monarch Book Company, 1898.

130   Isaac Murphy rode Kentucky Derby winners Buchanan in 1884, Riley in 1890, and Kingman in 1891.

131   1923 *City Directory* lists Hester Norton, residence 341 West Fourth; 1925 *City Directory* lists Hester Norton, saleslady, residence 562 Maryland.

131   *The Lexington Leader*, August 31, 1926.

139   There are two cancelled checks in the Jordan/Meadors collection made out to Miss Annice Poore, one dated August 11, 1902, for $18.00, and one dated December 8, 1902, for $4.00. Both checks were signed "Mrs. J. B. Kenney." We can only speculate that Miss Poore either did not know or did not wish it to be known that she was receiving checks from the infamous Belle Brezing.

139   Rent collections for Belle's rental property were made by John W. Stoll Company. A letter to Belle, dated September 19, 1931, shows the rent on the Dewees Street house was $30.00 a month. Stoll charged 10% commission.

139   "The Most Orderly of Disorderly Houses," page 5.

140   Belle did not even see McFarland about her financial affairs at the last before her death.

145   *The Lexington Leader*, August 12, 1940.

145   The cards were sent by Joseph C. Graves, Sr., a man known for his humor and given to practical jokes, who owned his own printing press.

146   *Highlights and Shadows*, volume 15, number 7, September, 1940.

147–149   *The Lexington Herald*, August 13, 1940, pages 1, 2. J. R. "Babe" Kimbrough, reporter; Tom Stone, photographer.

150   *The Lexington Leader*, August 21, 1940.

164   *The Lexington Herald*, August 23, 1940.

165   Mrs. Musser says women bought dresses and hats at the auction and wore them down the street.

167   State of Michigan in the Probate Court for the County of Wayne, In the Matter of Daisy Kenney, a Mentally Incompetent Person, No. 95,705.

168   Fayette Circuit Court, Daisy Kenney's Guardian (Committee), Plaintiff, vs. Daisy Kenney, Defendant, Notice to take Depositions, No. 25930.

Page

169   Deed Book 417, pages 438–439, Fayette County Courthouse.

169   Deed Book 326, pages 446–448, Fayette County Courthouse.

169   Fayette County Court, In the Matter of the Estate of Belle Breezing, Deceased: First and Final Settlement of Nolan Carter as Administrator of the Estate of Belle Breezing, Fayette County Courthouse, Book 41, pages 93–94.

169   Belle's Paris fashions sold for 25¢ and 50¢ each. Her bedroom slippers (still under the bed) went for a dime.

170   Certificate of Death, Michigan Department of Health, Bureau of Records and Statistics, State File No. 383809.

174   Clara Sayre related this story to a close personal friend. The episode has been mistakenly repeated in connection with Belle.

180   Among many copies of this well-known picture of Belle is a 4′ × 5′ reproduction on the wall at Lexington Mall. The coffee service in the photograph is now the proud possession of a Philadelphia lady.

The entire Thompson collection of Belle Brezing material will eventually be housed at the Margaret I. King Library, University of Kentucky Libraries.

Indictments

Dec. 14, 1882   Belle Breezing   charged with operating bawdy house; pardoned by Governor Luke B. Blackburn on Feb. 7, 1883

Jan. 11, 1884   Belle Breezing   indicted; filed away Dec. 15, 1885

June 10, 1884   Belle Breezing   indicted for maintaining a nuisance; fined $100 and costs Feb. 12, 1885

June 6, 1885   Belle Breezing   indicted for nuisance; filed away Dec. 15, 1885

Nov. 26, 1886   Belle Breezing   indicted for nuisance; fined $300 and costs Feb. 7, 1887

Dec. 16, 1887   Belle Breezing   indicted for tipling house; fined $100 and costs Feb. 6, 1888

June 8, 1888   Belle Breezing   indicted for tipling house; fined $60 and costs Nov. 19, 1888

Feb. 15, 1889   Belle Breezing   indicted for two nuisance charges; both filed away Nov. 18, 1889

Dec. 19, 1891   Belle Breezing   indicted for tipling house; fined $60 and costs Feb. 2, 1892

Dec. 17, 1892   Belle Breezing   indicted for unlawful sale of liquor; fined $20 and costs Feb. 15, 1893

Mar. 3, 1893   Belle Breezing   indicted for unlawful sale of liquor; trial in absence of defendant; jury verdict $150 and costs May 2, 1893

Oct. 5, 1893   Belle Breezing   indicted for unlawful sale of liquor; fined $150 and costs Dec. 5, 1893

Oct. 9, 1893   Belle Breezing   indicted for unlawful sale of liquor

Dec. 16, 1893   Belle Breezing   indicted for nuisance; filed away Feb. 11, 1894

Jul. 19, 1911   Belle Breezing   indicted for selling liquor without a license; selling to a minor, and selling on Sunday

COMMONWEALTH VS. BELLE BREEZING
GENERAL INDEX, COMMONWEALTH CAUSES, #1
CRIMINAL COURT RECORD
FAYETTE COUNTY COURTHOUSE

Box 72	1883
Box 78	1884
Box 83	1885
	1886
Box 93	1887
Box 101	1888
Box 110	1888
Box 115 (2 cases)	1889
	1890
Box 130	1891
	1892
Box 137	1893
Box 139	1893
Box 146 (2 cases)	1893
Box 148	1894
Box 197 (2 cases)	1902
Box 201	1903
Box 219	1910
Box 222 (3 cases)	1911
Box 232 (2 cases)	1914
Box 239	1915
	1916
Box 247	1917

In the course of research completed for this book, the following names of known prostitutes and madams have appeared in various documents and interviews. Most are probably assumed names.

Alice Allen (Debbie Harvey, Devonia Harvey, Alice Ely, Alice Roach)
Minnie Allen
F. Arnold
Belle Barnett (Belle Campbell)
Lillie Bell
Frances Belmont
Lue Bennett
Ann Bishop
Mother Board
Lillian Bowers
Lilly Bowman
Belle Brezing
Daisy Brooks
Belle Brown
Lottie Brown
Barb Burnell
Ada Caldwell
Belle Campbell (Belle Barnett)
May Cassidy
Ella Childers
Lizzie Church
Mamie Clayton
Margaret Combs
Matie Courtney
Mattie Crabtree
Ethel Cunningham
"Big Tit" Lil Davidson
Lizzie Davidson
Fannie Davis (Fannie Parshall)
Mayme Davis
Nellie Denhart
Nettie Denhart
Sarah Denney
Belle Dennis
May Dobbs
D. Dodson
Sue Downing
Mae Duncan
May Duncan
B. Edwards
Alice Ely (Debbie Harvey, Devonia Harvey, Alice Allen, Alice Roach)

Maud Fleming
Sallie Fleming
G. Foreman
Gene Gentry
M. Gill
Lilly Gofal
Eda Grant
Gertie Graves
Gussie Graves
Leta Graves
Rose Green (Rose Turner)
Sue Green
Julia Grinstead
Rebecca Hall
Laura Hampton
Debbie Harvey (Devonia Harvey, Alice Ely, Alice Allen, Alice Roach)
Devonia Harvey (Debbie Harvey, Alice Ely, Alice Allen, Alice Roach)
Emma Harvey
Lil Haverly
L. Hayes
Anna Hensley
Emma Hensley
Fannie Hensley
Frankie Hill
Jennie Hill
Lizzie Hill
Effie Howard
Bea Hudson
Mable Hughes
Pearl Hughes
Fannie Hustey
Beatrice Huston
Mollie Irvine
Mary Jackson (Blanche Patterson)
Blanche Johnson
M. Johnson
Maude Jones
Phoebe Jones
Lillie Kahn
Florence Kaufman
Mollie Kennedy

Clara Kessler (Clara Sayre)
Rose Kincaid
Rose Kinkead
S. Laugham
Grace Lawrence
Georgie Lee
Ethel Leon
Gerty Lisle
Ena Livingston
Grace Long
Mollie Long
Mag Lyons
Hannah McAfee
Mary McCarthy
Ethel McQuire
Ethal Maguirer
Fannie Marshall
Frances Marshall
Mayst Martfield (Marjorie
    Mayfield)
Eda Martin
Ida Martin
Goldie May
Marjorie Mayfield (Mayst
    Martfield)
Inez Meyers
Sallie Moore
Dolly Morgan
Almeda Mukes
Mamie Murphy
Lilly Nunnelly
Cora Odon
Mag Oliver
B. Palm
Molly Parker
Fannie Parshall (Fannie Davis)
Blanche Patterson (Mary Jackson)
Lizzie Patterson
Lettie Powell

Sallie Price
Alice Roach (Debbie Harvey,
    Devonia Harvey, Alice Allen,
    Alice Ely)
? Robinson
Jasie Roe
Josie Roe
Lulu Rose
A. Ross
Fannie Rule
Clara Sayre (Clara Kessler)
Mina Sayre
Grace Shea
"Snooky" Simpson
A. M. Smith
Margaret Spears
Bertha Steele
Dile Stone
Lila Stone
Matie Stone
Emma Strange
Maud Surville
Carrie Taylor
Pink Thomas
Rose Turner (Rose Green)
J. Ollie Van Gordon
Ruby Veit
Mattie Wade
Mattie Waid
Mary Walker
Emma Walters
Lillian Ward
Nell Welch
Julia White
Annie Williams
Tessie Williams
Frankie Wright
Pearl Wright
Ray Young

Illustration Credits

Pages 16, 175, Herbie Feeback, Jr., Collection; page 17, J. Winston Coleman, Jr., Kentuckiana Collection, Transylvania University Library; pages 44, 54, 144, 151, John C. Wyatt; page 81, Miriam Tuska Collection; page 120, A. C. Stagg Stamp Collection. All other illustrations from author's collection.